FOG IN CHANNEL ...?

FOG IN CHANNEL...?

Exploring Britain's Relationship with Europe

Compiled and edited by
Tom Sykes and Simon Sykes

shoehorn
www.shoehornbooks.com

Dedication

The late Lieutenant Commander R "Bill" Sykes, RN

Acknowledgements

We would like to thank all our contributors for their involvement, encouragement and patience throughout this project. We would also like to thank our publisher, Simon Rix, at Shoehorn for his friendly enthusiasm, advice and efficiency in getting the book to publication.

Shoehorn Current Affairs & History Books

Published by
Shoehorn Media Ltd
4 Great Marlborough Street
London W1F 7HH
England
www.shoehornbooks.com

First published in 2009.

A CIP catalogue record for this book is available from the British Library.

ISBNs: 978-1-907149-06-1 (hard back) 978-1-907149-07-8 (paper back)

Printed in the UK by LSUK, Milton Keynes.

Cover photograph courtesy of NASA.

Contents

Introduction

We began compiling this book in 2004 as a means of exploring the UK's relationship with Europe through the thoughts and feelings of people from various backgrounds and from all sides of the political spectrum. We hope that this compilation of written and graphic pieces will be a compelling, useful and informative contribution to a vitally important debate.

Rather than offering detailed analysis of the specific policies and mechanisms of the EU, this project investigates deeper issues of culture, experience, social interaction and value systems as they relate to a more profound conception of Europe as an historical, geographical and psychological entity. Such policies and mechanisms are already much written about and perhaps it seems that the more they are discussed, in whatever medium, the less engaged in practical terms we all become; we grow indifferent to the myriad interpretations of policy; we weary of the dry debates on systems; we disengage and are confused. Thus, we feel we have taken a more personal and human approach than other publications in this field, providing an antidote to all those textbooks, reports and pamphlets that are perhaps too dull and academic to properly enthuse the public.

Above all, we hope that this book will have a practical use, encouraging people to engage more fully with and think more constructively about the future of the UK and of Europe.

We welcome any comments from readers - please contact us on ficcco@hotmail.com.

Tom Sykes and Simon Sykes 2009

Charles Kennedy
President of the European Movement and former leader of the Liberal Democrats

Europe: A Federal Future

Notwithstanding the easy political soundbites of 'the worst economic downturn for a hundred years', no-one can say with any seriousness that the challenges we face are of a greater order of magnitude than those which confronted Jean Monnet and his contemporaries.

They faced the reality of a continent devastated by war, its industries smashed, its people displaced, its future uncertain as a new age of ideological confrontation dawned. Yet even in such bleak circumstances, it was Monnet who managed to transform what on paper were pragmatic economic exercises – such as the European Coal and Steel Community and the Common Market – into the beacons of a nascent European ideal.

He sought to transcend our parochialisms – not to sacrifice what is different about us, but to draw strength from that which unites us.

That is why our European future must be a federal one – of states bound together by common ambitions as much as legal treaties. Monnet knew that in the dark years of postwar reconstruction his beloved France could not act alone.

In these years of economic turmoil, climate change and the threat of international terrorism, the same can be said of us.

Britain alone does not have the answer to economic stagnation, nor global terrorism nor – most fundamentally of all – how to save our planet. This last challenge is the greatest we face, yet in the aftermath of a bank collapse or a terrorist atrocity, often drifts out of the 'here and now' into the 'sometime in the future.' That's not good enough. And the only way we can maintain our focus – on all the diverse challenges that threaten us at once – is to do so together.

This is our federal future – of states bound together by a shared purpose – by a shared consciousness of what is important to us, by a shared statement of how we wish to act to preserve justice and freedom around the world.

The fate of the global economy is naturally uppermost in people's minds. After a decade of politics – in many countries – which has abounded with the rhetoric of choice but, locked in the iron grip of an economic consensus, has often failed to offer any, our response has been purely reactive.

Saving the financial system was an action which needed little debate; political point-scoring here leaves a still-sourer taste than usual. But so far the publics of the European Union have looked to it for concerted action in vain. Point-scoring has not been limited to national parities, but to international finger-jabbing, with one set of finance ministers desperate to convince their electorate that they have performed better than their European rivals in their handling of the crisis. This is not the spirit of a shared solution to our problems.

Naturally Britain, which remains outside the Eurozone, has a greater necessity for unilateral action. And naturally Britain, being in this position, is tempted by a return to economic nationalism.

For anyone who doubts the politics of nationalism are alive and well, take a look at the events at the Lindsey Oil Refinery in Lincolnshire. The rhetoric was familiar, and unappealing – foreign workers 'taking' British jobs, which the prime minister had apparently promised to 'British workers'. In short – when the going gets tough, do we simply abandon our principles of free trade and the free movement of labour, which in the long run have brought us economic growth and peaceful stability?

Portuguese and Italian workers have a right to work here. Just as British workers have a right to work in Portugal and Italy. And I believe that this offers benefits for our societies which far outweigh the basic realities of economic need.

Yet even when the times weren't tough, the spectre of economic nationalism – and the often xenophobic politics which accompanies it – has often loomed in the background of public discourse about Europe. But there are sound economic reasons why it must be rejected, as Juan Manuel Barroso put it in 2006:

> "… it is the Community law that gives us the legitimacy and the grounds to speak out and explain why economic nationalism is wrong. To explain that defending national champions in the short-term, usually ends up relegating them to the second division in the long-term, and to generally create unrest between member states … A pan-European market needs pan-European champions … slipping backwards into … mini-markets would be the highest folly, not just because of increasing global competition, but because it would mean the beginning of the end of the European project itself." [1]

The consequences of falling back into that parochialism would be catastrophic for Britain, and for Europe as a whole. That's why I believe that now we must reconsider our position on the Euro. I have said before that joining the Euro cannot be a policy, but it must be a strategy. With the tumultuous times we face over the course of the next year and a half, it is not feasible for Britain to enter the monetary union before the next General Election.

But Euro entry must once again become a touchstone of our political debate on the economy. It would bind us to the interests we share with our European partners, and help prevent fratricidal economic measures which would gain no victory. More than this, it would provide new possibilities when growth returns; the challenge for us will be to be ready.

We also need now to get beyond the Lisbon agenda. This may require creativity in our thinking, and determination in our actions. I cannot stress enough that when I say 'get beyond' I do not mean simply impose the will of the Commission or any other body on the

---

[1] JM Barroso, 'Uniting in Peace: The role of law in the European Union', Jean Monnet Lecture, European University Institute, Florence, 31 March 2006, page 7.

populations of the member states. I mean we must have the debate, so we can finish the process and concentrate on what Europe should be *doing* rather than *defining*. But we must have it swiftly – and we must not seek to pull the wool over the eyes of the electorate; we must be clear on what it is we aim to achieve and how it will help them – and how it will bring us closer together.

My idea of a federal future rests on a plethora of states with a unanimity of purpose. But whilst the darkness of the times calls for pan-European responses, it also calls for global ones – above and beyond the sphere of the economy. Whilst much of the global economy's present difficulties had their origins in the United States, undoubtedly they will also have the beginnings of their solutions there. The same might be said in the realm of foreign policy.

For the last few months, we have been transfixed by events in the United States. For many of us, those of us who have been critics of much of the substance of American foreign policy in the last eight years, these have been moments of hope and trepidation. Hope – that president Obama can make a decisive break with the past, and seize this opportunity to restore the United States' moral authority in the eyes of the world. And trepidation – the fear that this moment, in the face of all the challenges ourselves and our allies face, might be squandered.

When Barack Obama declared his intention to seek the presidency two years ago, he could not have anticipated the scale of the challenges he faces today. The prevailing global economic crisis structures all debate. When he penned an essay in *Foreign Affairs* in July 2007,[2] outlining his foreign policy prospectus as a potential future American president, financial and economic woes were nowhere to be seen. All that has changed. While the world still holds the president to his past promises, to his pledge to bring the Iraq War to a close, to his decision – happily already made – to close Guantanamo and bring to an end American support for torture, he now faces a new foreign policy environment where economic and material needs dominate the agenda. His room for maneouvre is limited, as is ours. European nations throughout the Union have

[2] Barack Obama, 'Renewing American Leadership', *Foreign Affairs*, July/August, 2007.

become inward-looking, desperate to shore up economies struck by the credit crunch, desperate to restore confidence to publics in a state of shock.

Nowhere is this more true than in Britain, where the IMF believes the hardest blows will fall. My country – often against my wishes! - has been the most ardent of America's military allies in the last decade. Yet even Britain, with one of the highest publicly declared percentage spends on its military, is over-stretched and facing severe cutbacks to her Armed Forces, including severe reductions in the Royal Navy's surface fleet and its ability to project power overseas. These reductions come even as the UK has committed herself to leading the first EU maritime anti-piracy operation in the Horn of Africa.

As president Obama himself noted, America's ability to project hard power has also been reduced – both by stretch and by the damage done to the Department of Defense under former secretary Rumsfeld. It remains to be seen whether his proposal of military expansion remains a viable possibility in an era of domestic belt-tightening. It might, in the circumstances, seem well that the new president's emphasis is on soft, rather than hard power; that secretary Clinton has already committed her State Department to the forging of alliances that will replace the unilateralism of the past. And it is welcome. It is to be hoped that gone are the days when the American government viewed the advice of its European allies simply as an apology for self-interest or indifference to global issues.

Yet the need for strong armed forces – in the United States and in Europe – has not disappeared. Even as both Britain and the United States prepare to leave Iraq, a real war is being waged in Afghanistan, an intervention which – unlike Iraq – did command international support; but which has seen a disproportionate burden placed on the United States and Britain in terms of warfighting – and casualties. And hard power is the unspoken subtext to soft power – the knowledge that diplomacy, while always the first choice, is never the last resort in the face of danger.

But more vital still is unity of purpose, and we in Europe have a key role to fulfil.

For – in the last decade – our house has been divided. Notwithstanding the Common Foreign and Security Policy, there has been little unanimity between member states on how to deal with the most pressing security concerns of our time.

Britain, Spain and Poland all committed troops to the Iraq conflict. France, Germany and many other nations were passionately opposed. Leaving aside the rights and wrongs of either position, let us face the fact that an EU divided on matters of such critical importance can hardly be an effective force. What we need in Europe is a redefined foreign policy strategy; a commitment to cooperation made real within our own Union before we engage in foreign adventures overseas.

Divisions such as these undermine our ability to deploy soft power – to be credible diplomats – for years to come. And our ability to use soft power will determine our ability to respond to the challenges we face.

First among these must be the continuing conflict in Afghanistan. As a legitimate intervention which pledged to bring democracy to a country under the yoke of theocracy, whether we succeed or fail there will send a clear signal to our enemies and those who might wish to prey on the weakness of the Atlantic alliance.

Despite changing political cultures, European nations have often been unwilling to play their full part in the struggle waged there. Words must be translated into actions – not merely by some nations in the Union, but by all. The recent conflict in Gaza has also reiterated the need for a strong position not merely on the part of the Quartet – but on the part of the EU itself – in any attempt to restore dialogue. In part, this must mean negotiating with those we have previously found it impossible to talk to.

We cannot finance elections and simply declare the result unsatisfactory – as we did in the election of Hamas. It is not enough for the High Representative, Javier Solana, to meet with president Abbas and argue that Hamas be elbowed out of the picture. If we truly believe in democracy, we must be prepared to abide by its results.

For those who say there can be no negotiation with Hamas while they refuse to recognise Israel, I say this; the British government was prepared to negotiate in secret with the IRA even when that organisation espoused the destruction of any United Kingdom of Great Britain and Northern Ireland. It is necessary to talk to those with influence, not merely ostracise them in the hope that they will see the error of their ways.

This is just as appropriate in terms of the Iranian government as towards the leadership of Hamas. President Obama's attempts to reach out to Tehran have been well-documented. Iran cannot be allowed to become a pariah state, beyond the reach of the international order, nuclear armed and unwilling to cooperate with neigbours, yet only too willing to threaten Israel.

This would be a tragedy for the whole of the Middle East, not merely for Iran. We must be prepared to join with the United States in an approach of constructive engagement with Tehran, and to act as intermediaries in the warming of a relationship which has been cool for far too long.

The recent crisis in Georgia has highlighted the continuing difficulties in our relationship with Russia. European energy security is imperilled by any deterioration in Russo-European relations, dependent as much of continental Europe is on Russian gas supplies. The sense of powerlessness felt by many in Europe during the Georgia conflict emphasised the real dificulties this assymetric relationship has created.

Georgia, a nation-state friendly to the EU and on the road to NATO membership, found herself in a war with a much stronger power and with no realistic possibility of help from her new allies. The impotence of European leaders and foreign ministers will have reinforced the belief in Moscow that the EU is weak and an inadequate bulwark against Russian ambitions.

Yet only last month president Medvedev's decision to withold stationing missiles in Eastern Europe has shown the possibilities for constructive engagement which the Obama presidency represents. We must be prepared to play our part – in any way possible – to aid in the deescalation of tensions.

The European Union is at its best when addressing challenges that go beyond borders. The threat of global warming and consequent climate change must rank amongst the most profound of these. There is a danger – when we live in times of economic turmoil – that this may fall from the political agenda, but instead we must retain the EU as the beacon of how to tackle climate change, in order to lead the world on an issue which will have dire consequences for our children's children. This is a key reason why our economic polices must remain in concert, and not represent parochial responses to issues of global importance.

We must find once again the most fundamental ground that unites all of us; in president Kennedy's words, 'that we all breathe the same air; that we are all human.'

Our Union had its origins in a post-war desire to foster greater cooperation and solidarity between nations that had seen too much of war and crisis. While the challenges we face may not yet be as stark as those our nations faced during 1939-1945, or indeed during the Cold War which followed, they are no less real, and in the long term, far more dangerous. For the first time in a decade, an American president resides in the White House who is not merely content but willing to engage on the global stage in a manner beyond simple condescension and threat.

For some of the challenges we face, notably climate change, the impact of which at times seems remote, it is not possible to wait any longer. We need the United States to adopt an emissions trading scheme on the European model; we need the United States to lead, so that developing countries dependent on fossil fuels will not be confounded by the hypocrisy of the West.

We need to act now – because ecological realities will not wait for the restoration of the world financial system and the resumption of economic 'normality'.

We need, as Europeans, to rediscover that unifying spirit of our own founding fathers, to look for our common humanity both in this continent and beyond, and to reform our Union so we can seize the chance to join with our global partners in this moment of profound significance.

That is what I mean by our federal future – of a unity of purpose, enshrined in a framework of a nation states no longer concerned exclusively with naval-gazing at the minutiae of treaties and the form – rather than the content – of Europe. We have a long way to go.

President Obama noted that the United States had stood aside while atrocities were perpetrated in Zimbabwe and genocide in Rwanda. We were no less guilty.

Though we cannot seek peace in the world without the aid of the United States, we cannot always simply shrug our shoulders and look to America. In Afghanistan, we must all shoulder our share of the burden. In Darfur – and in the Darfurs of the future – we must make it clear that this Union will live up to its own foreign policy and reserve the right to act in line with the UN Charter. We will require more credible armed forces to do this. But we will also require a more credible sense of purpose. This purpose – built on a federal Europe - will inform not merely our foreign policy, but our shared economic interests, and our response to the challenge of climate change.

These challenges we face today offer an opportunity for us to remake Europe in the fight for a prosperous future. It asks only for us to seize it.

Edwin Morgan

Poet

In one loose sense I can be called a European in that I have visited many European countries: France, Germany, the Netherlands, Belgium, Austria, Norway, Sweden, Finland, Iceland, Ukraine, Hungary, Italy, Czechoslovakia, Poland, Russia, Romania and Turkey. I am interested in languages, and the European patchwork of very different languages has a great fascination, even if it seems to make a United States of Europe problematic from the start.

European culture is old and impressive; you can hardly move for classics. At the same time, Britain is an offshore island complex which (like Japan at the other side of Eurasia) will never become an integral part of Europe, despite the Channel Tunnel. Its association with Europe will always be qualified or provisional or strained, simply through geography. There will always be treaties but I doubt if they can go 100 percent of the way.

A further interesting complication: I live in Scotland, the most northerly part of these islands and (to put it another way) the furthest from London and its influence. Yesterday there was an official opening of the remarkable new building of the Scottish Parliament. 'The UK' has become considerably weakened by the establishment of a Welsh Assembly and a Scottish Parliament, and a Scottish view of Europe will not necessarily chime with an English view of Europe. The UKIP will make few inroads in Scotland. And again: those living in Edinburgh, on the east coast, face Europe, but those (like myself) living in Glasgow, on the west coast, face America. American influence, strong in Glasgow, cuts across any simple pro- or anti- Europe position. I have been to various parts of America, from New York to San Francisco, and have found it impossible to be immune from the vigour and forward-looking of the country, even while being unsympathetic to American hegemony and imperialism. By comparison, Europe can sometimes look as if it did not care if history was passing it by. As a believer in progress, I find this worrying. None of this makes for easy decisions.

I have probably done no more than air the problems, but I think it is useful to identify them, as against a clasping of slogans and skiing downhill to some terminal moraine.

Tony Benn
Writer and socialist

Some people believe that we shall never get social justice from the British Government, but we shall get it from the European Union. They believe that a good king is better than a bad parliament. I have never taken that view. Others believe that the change is inevitable, and that the common currency will protect us from inflation and will provide a wage policy. None of those arguments persuade me because the argument has never been about sovereignty.

I do not know what a sovereign is, apart from the one that used to be in gold and the Pope who is a sovereign in the Vatican. We are talking about democracy. No nation – not even the great United States which could, for all I know, be destroyed by a nuclear weapon from a third-world country – has the power to impose its will on other countries. We are discussing whether the British people are to be allowed to elect those who make the laws under which they are governed.

I know that it sounds negative but I have always thought it positive to say that the important thing about democracy is that we can remove without bloodshed the people who govern us. But that cannot be done in the structure of the EU. Even if one likes the policies of the people in Europe, one cannot get rid of them.

I say to my favourite friends, the Chartists and suffragettes, 'All your struggles to get control of the ballot box were a waste of time. We shall be run in future by a few white persons, as in 1832.' The instrument, I might add, is the Royal Prerogative of treaty making. For the first time since 1649 the crown makes the laws – advised, I admit, by the prime minister.

If people lose the power to sack their Government, one of several things happens. First, people may just slope off. Apathy could destroy democracy. When the turnout drops below 50 percent, we are in danger...

The second thing that people can do is to riot. Riot is an old-fashioned method for drawing the attention of the Government to what is wrong. It is difficult for an elected person to admit it, but the riot at Strangeways for example, produced some prison reforms. Riot has historically played a much larger part in British politics than we are ever allowed to know.

Thirdly, nationalism can arise. Instead of blaming the Treaty of Rome, people say, 'It is those Germans' or 'It is the French'. Nationalism is built out of frustration that people feel when they cannot get their way through the ballot box. With nationalism comes repression. I hope that it is not pessimistic – in my view it is not – to say that democracy hangs by a thread in every country of the world. Unless we can offer people a peaceful route to the resolution of injustices through the ballot box, they will not listen to a Parliament that has blocked off that route.

There are many alternatives open to us for a new Europe. But there have already been five Europes this century. There was one run by the King, the Kaiser and the Tsar – they were all cousins so that was very comfortable. They were all Queen Victoria's grandsons. And there was no nonsense about human rights when Queen Victoria's grandsons repressed people. Then there was the Russian Revolution. Then there was the inter-war period. Then there was the Anglo-Soviet alliance. Then there was the Cold War. Now we have an administration in Russia who seems to have joined the Monday Club. There have been many Europes. This is not the only Europe on offer.

I understand the position of the democratic federalists. They want an American-type constitution for Europe. It could be that our laws hang on which way the Albanian members voted. I could not complain about that because it is democracy. However, it is unworkable. It is like trying to get an elephant to dance through a minefield. But it would be democratic.

Another way would be to have a looser, wider Europe. I have an idea for a Commonwealth of Europe. Europe would be rather like the British Commonwealth. We would work by consent with people. Or we could accept this ghastly proposal, which is clumsy, secretive, centralised, bureaucratic and divisive. That is how I regard the Treaty of Rome. I was born a European and I will die one. But I have never put my alliance behind the Treaty of Rome. I object to it. I hate being called an anti-European. How can one be anti-European when one is born in Europe? It is like saying that one is anti-British if one does not agree with the Chancellor of the Exchequer. What a lot of nonsense it is.

Parliament has lost confidence in democracy. It believes that it must be governed by someone else. It is afraid to use the powers entrusted to it by its constituents. It has traded power for status. One gets asked to go on the telly if one is a member of parliament. Parliament does not want to use its power. It has accepted the role of a spectator and joined what Bagehot called the dignified part of the constitution, leaving the Crown, under the control of the prime minister, to be the Executive part.

If democracy is destroyed in Britain it will not be the communists, Trotskyists or subversives but Parliament which threw it away. The rights that are entrusted to MPs are not for them to give away. It is theft of public rights.

Mine is not a nationalist argument nor is it about sovereignty. It is a democratic argument.

Dr Azzam Tamimi
Director of the Institute of Islamic Political Thought in London

Exercise Your Right; Perform Your Duty, Vote!

Muslim citizens of European Union states today have an unprecedented opportunity to influence politics and decision-making across the continent. On the one hand, the number of Muslims eligible to vote is higher than ever, while on the other, a broader common ground than ever exists today where Muslims and non-Muslims may stand together and work jointly in order to bring politicians to account on both domestic and international policies. From a religious standpoint Muslims are expected to play an active role in elections at all levels, European, national and local, since this is one of the most effective means of implementing two central Islamic principles: enjoining the good and forbidding the evil; and cooperating in accomplishing *birr* (the good and noble) and *taqwa* (piety and righteousness). A Muslim person who has the right to vote bears two responsibilities: he or she must first have the determination to use his or her voting power with the intention of accomplishing the good and avoiding the evil; secondly, he or she must use that power in the right way so that, to the best of a voter's knowledge, good is sought and evil is avoided.

Until recently, few Muslims took elections seriously and those that did tended to make little effort to vote for the right candidate. Those that did not participate at all thought it did not matter or make a difference or thought it was *haram* (forbidden). In both cases, a grave error of judgment is made and a great loss is therefore incurred.

As for the first case, it is a fact that every vote in an election counts. Evidently, candidates never cease to hunt for votes and do not rest until the ballot boxes are sealed. Effectively, it does not matter by how many votes a seat is won. Particularly the votes of minorities in a milieu infected with 'majority' apathy become extremely valuable and do indeed make a huge difference.

As for the second case, it is only right for a Muslim to want to find out the position of Shari'ah on an unprecedented situation. Indeed, the presence of Muslims in Europe is a new phenomenon. Therefore, it is only natural that such Muslims would face challenges that earlier Muslims did not face and were not therefore addressed by scholars of earlier times. However, that does not mean that answers to new questions are not or cannot be found. Thanks to the process of *ijtihad* the scholars of each time and place endeavour to provide answers and respond to new situations. Just as a doctor would do when diagnosing a complaint, the *fuqaha* (scholars who are experts in Islamic jurisprudence) look thoroughly into the matter under consideration and refer to a set of agreed upon rules before they issue a *fatwa* (informed opinion).

No excuse remains today for Muslims who live in Europe, or in other similar situations where they constitute a minority, not to participate in politics and take part in elections. Leading Muslim scholars worldwide have dealt with this matter and clarified the Shari'ah on this matter. Here in Europe we have had a detailed explanation in the form of a *fatwa* issued by the European Council of Fatwa, which is headed by Sheikh Yusuf Al-Qaradawi. The Council includes among its members a number of leading Muslim scholars from within and outside Europe. In brief, the position of these leading scholars is that the condition of a Muslim minority living in a non-Muslim country is considered an exception to the rule. The rule under normal circumstances is that a Muslim community should seek to lead a life guided by Islam whether in private or in public – including governance. However, whenever this is not possible a community should seek more good and prevent more evil. Such a responsibility is both individual and collective. The fact that in certain circumstances not all 'good' can be accomplished nor all 'evil' can be averted, does exempt Muslims from shouldering this responsibility.

Muslim men and women living in Europe as citizens who have voting rights can, and should endeavour to, make a difference by exercising their voting rights or, one may say, by applying their voting power. Claims by some individuals or fringe groups that this would be *haram* are simply false. Such claims are either due to ignorance or some hidden agenda whose purpose is to disempower the Muslims and render them useless. This is exactly what should be characterised as *haram*.

Furthermore, what is truly *haram* is allowing bad politicians to get away with unjust and erroneous policies while we have the opportunity to stop them or replace them. It would indeed be sinful for a Muslim man or woman to refrain from making an effort that would, if exerted, result in improving things for Islam, Muslims and humanity. It is sinful for a Muslim to deceive other Muslims by claiming to have knowledge while lacking it and to discourage them from having a say when that say matters and is greatly needed!

Bill Deedes (1913-2007)
Journalist

My attitude to the UK's relationship to Europe is too brief to be worth printing. I was born in 1913, eve of the calamitous First World War, the ill consequences and losses of which are still with us today. It cost our best stock. Look at any village memorial.

Barely had we buried the dead from that one and held inquests on the mass slaughter battles such as Somme and Dardanelles, we were at it again, requiring some of us to give five years of our life to fighting. More good stock down the drain.

The European Community with all its faults, weaknesses, corruption and itch for power over our lives offers this generation and its young a better prospect than 1914-18 and 1939-45. However hard it tried it couldn't be any worse! So I support it.

Ralph Steadman

Cartoonist

Zoe Readhead

Principal, Summerhill School and daughter of its founder, AS Neill

I deal with many European parents and kids here at Summerhill. I love the feeling of being a 'European' but so do I love the feeling of being a 'worldean'. I love that we are all sharing a world (sadly not very harmoniously) and that we are diverse and different. I would hate France to become less French and England to become less English – let's keep the Italians Italian and the Spaniards Spanish. I miss foreign money – the Euro is so impersonal – and I still use inches, feet and ounces.

I like the European support for Human Rights and sensible things like that – but I would like to keep our own personal government power (if only it was one that could be trusted) to deal with our own issues. I don't like the way so many things (even down to our local small slaughter houses which were individual and humane) have been gobbled up by the European Union – and look with alarm at how more and more things seem to disappear. I think the EU should be more a support group than a governing group.

Steve Nallon

Impressionist, actor, writer and broadcaster

www.nallon.com

I know it's an old story, but it goes something like this. A French mayor greets a British delegation and welcomes them to his charming and beloved Normandy village. His speech includes the popular local expression *espirit de Normandie*, a phrase summing up the warmness of the Normandy people. However, when this idiomatic expression is translated into English by the French translator for the mono-linguistic British delegation, they all burst out laughing. French pride is affronted. *Why all deese British Beefies to be mocking of our friendly salutation?* Well, all is revealed when it is explained that the French into English translation of *espirit de Normandie* became somewhat literally expressed as, "Ladies and gentlemen, I greet you in the name of Norman Wisdom." Good job that movie icon Norman Wisdom – the nearest Britain ever got to that French comic genius Jacques Tati – was a clown familiar to at least some of the French villagers.

Clearly translation in the EU doesn't always translate. Even my 'alternative' Mrs T, just like the Normandy mayor, also discovered that. In the 1980s I worked on the satirical puppet series *Spitting Image*, providing the voice of the then prime minister Margaret Hilda Thatcher. I also occasionally dressed up as 'Lady M'. My alter ego version of the PM was particularly popular when 'she' popped up at business conferences in Britain. Occasionally, she also crossed the English Channel promoting British companies in Europe.

On one occasion I attended a conference in Brussels to make a presentation to a group of EU delegates. I forget for which company. The idea was to add a bit of humour to an otherwise dull day. Most delegates were non-English speaking, or at least they preferred to rely on the simultaneous translation rather than their own knowledge of the English language.

My concern wasn't just how English jokes would go down – would the European delegates, for example, have the knowledge of the British class system to get Mrs T's ironic throwaway comment "I was in the north of England this week in Watford"? No, I was also concerned about the translation. How would it work going from your actual English into your actual French, German, Dutch and so on? You see, many of my jokes depended on the flexibility of the English language to mean two things at once. I often, for example, would have Maggie mixing up her metaphors. Her confused combinations of homilies would include a not too hidden double entendre: "As I said to the German Chancellor, 'Yes! I am prepared to negotiate! So, as the saying goes, *if you play ball with me – I'll scratch yours!*" I was told not to worry, everything would be fine, though be prepared, they said, for the Germans, who were known for laughing at jokes just that little bit behind everyone else. And laughing in silence.

I began my speech – "Now, I suppose you are all wondering why I sent for you." Three seconds later a smile appeared on an array of faces beneath headsets simultaneously translating me word by word. "Some of you I know personally – others of you I just have files on." A titter closely followed. "Of course, I look forward, at the next G7 meeting in Britain, to welcoming all the important world leaders – and president Mitterand." Two seconds later, a burst of giggles. Even from the French. It was going very well. I continued to time the speech in such a way that, even taking into account people getting the joke after I said it and via another voice, no one felt left out or left behind.

Margaret's husband, Denis, was always a popular part of my act back in the 1980s. He was a comedy turn in his own right, with his fondness for golf and his ever present bottle of gin. Jokes in these areas were becoming a bit obvious so I also developed a somewhat surreal routine that included Margaret proudly boasting about Denis's wartime exploits. I was dubious about doing this routine at all outside Britain but the organisers said no one would be offended. It would be seen as a joke on Thatcher not on any one else.

I had invented Denis's wartime heroics mainly on the premise that he was his regiment's Chief Laundry Officer. Denis's war effort was cleanliness! So thorough in his duty to cleanliness was Denis that he *boiled* all vests, under garments and smalls. "Yes," Mrs T would say proudly, "Denis spent his time in the army joyously cooking socks." Now, said quickly, this can sound like something else. In fact to someone else it did sound like something else and that someone else was the German translator.

I'm told that in the old days the manual type-setters of newspaper printing presses were quicker if they were illiterate because then, as they were putting the old metal letter type into the press, they wouldn't waste time in actually reading copy: letters went it, letters went out with very little meaning. I suspect translators must sometimes work in a similar way: one word comes in the head and another goes out the mouth. What the word and its translation means perhaps isn't always grasped in the detail. The misheard phrase *Denis spent his time in the army joyously cooking socks* was I think such an occasion. Not heard as "cooking socks" but as something else and translated as such in the most unambiguous manner left the German delegation utterly helpless with laughter. Of course, I didn't know what I had said to make them laugh, for what they had heard was not what I had, actually. Still, it didn't take me long to work out.

Whether I had helped or hindered EU co-operation I do not know. However, it changed my perspective on the Germans. From then on I would never ask rhetorically – *Where would we be without a sense of humour?* and then reply to my own question with the answer ... *GERMANY!* No, the Germans have a very acute sense of humour, especially concerning the husband of a certain British PM and his wartime exploits. I doubt though the same sense of humour could be said to be had by the wartime hero's wife.

Peter Luff
Chairman, The European Movement
Director, Action for a Global Climate Community

Europe for me has always been personal: uncles fighting in two world wars – one gassed on Armistice Day 1918 telling his sister, my mother, as he died that the sacrifice was worth it because he had experienced the 'war to end all wars' and was certain that the circumstances could never arise again that would require his youngest brother to face the horrors of war. Just over two decades later, that brother was to fight for the free French in North Africa and in the Italian campaign, participating in the bloodbath of Monte Cassino and the liberation of Koblenz, where he was to meet his future wife – a young German woman, who had survived the retribution of the Red Army. Other uncles served in the British first and eighth armies and my father was in RAF ground control guiding in the planes that returned and, many years later, still mourning the crews of those that did not return. My maternal grandparents, were refugees from Belgium in the first war – my grandfather finding a temporary home for the paper he was editing in Fleet Street and then, as a writer on Hitler's blacklist, seeking refuge with his wife in the strip of France that was not directly occupied by the Nazis. They had all experienced the result of Europe's atavistic inability to break free of its fratricidal obsession and shared a common belief that the only hope for a lasting peace was a mature, self aware and united Europe able to settle its differences peacefully without resorting to the battlefields.

If this idea was planted firmly in my mind as I grew up, it was confirmed when I worked professionally for Amnesty International. It was there that I realised the central and crucial requirement of 'the rule of law' if the poor, the weak, the disenfranchised, the powerless and the disaffected were to have any hope of protection from the arbitrary cruelty and violence of not only dictators but hostile majorities. Only with guaranteed constitutional rights and the ability to seek redress in independent courts, can the inviolability of the citizen be guaranteed. Without a legal system legitimised through the democratic process and administered by an independent judiciary respected by the people it serves, individuals and minorities can never feel safe.

It was these two fundamental concepts – the need to find a system of international relations that could guarantee peace in Europe and the importance of the rule of law as a guarantee of human rights – that led me to understand and appreciate the extraordinary and unique historical importance of European integration. But there was one further piece of the jigsaw that I only fully appreciated after I became immersed in the development of the European Union as director of the European Movement UK, which was the underlying logic and political strength implicit in the notion of federalism.

It is an abiding mystery why the British, who recognised how federalism could reconcile national unity with the problems created by cultural, economic and geographical diversity in former colonies, appear unable to understand its application in the European context. The argument against has always been focussed on the dilution of national sovereignty, but not only is this only one part of the complex distribution of powers inherent in federalism, it is increasingly obvious that the problems facing not just Europe, indeed the whole world, today require a common vision and a unified approach. And, if a federal world may still seem inconceivable to many, the example of Europe at least blazes the trail and shows that it is conceivable that historical enemies can, in the right circumstances, embrace common political, legal and financial structures. The thought of Germany and France sharing a common parliament was as implausible to my grandparents' generation as common institutions for Israel and the rest of the Middle East today.

The British people have never been seriously offered a vision of Europe beyond something that might appeal to their immediate financial advantage. In fact, the momentum towards integration grew out of a far deeper realisation that no lasting advance – economic, political or social – can be achieved without preserving peace. And peace can only survive if a creative balance can be struck between the unifying process and rightful national and regional aspirations. The political philosophy devised to maintain that balance is federalism. This was recognised at the very start by Europe's founding fathers. Federalism has been at the heart of the move towards European unity since the creation of the Coal and Steel Community in 1952. Indeed, The Schuman Declaration of 1950 states unequivocally that, *'The pooling of coal and steel production should immediately provide for the setting up of common foundations for economic development as a first step in the federation of Europe ...'*

The lack of coherence in today's European Union does not lie in the failure to implement federalism but rather in the determination of national political elites to retain power in their own hands. But this is an illusion. The real threat to national sovereignty does not come neither from Brussels bureaucrats and even less from the European Parliament but from trans-national corporations, whose activities are increasingly uncontrollable by national legislation alone.

It is the desire of national political elites to cling on to the illusion of authority as well as their failure to consult their electorates about what they want from the process that poses the greatest threat to European integration. The European ideal requires constant restating and revising if it is to capture generations for whom European war has no personal resonance. There are good and clear arguments for the need to deepen the process of economic, monetary and political engagement and to extend the borders of the Union but they most certainly have not been explained to those European constituents for whom the free movement of goods, capital and people appears to threaten their employment and livelihood. Far too frequently, it has been assumed that the long-term benefits, including the importance of safeguarding democracy in newly liberated countries of Central and Eastern Europe, would be automatically understood but the reality that has emerged from the rejection of the constitution in France, Holland and elsewhere is that not only must the link be clearly explained but that the underlying reason for unity in an insecure world must be reaffirmed in a way that is relevant in today's political climate.

Most crucially, there is a growing cynicism on the part of electorates throughout Europe towards the political establishment in all the member states, which is increasingly justified. The recent referenda on the draft constitution was an enormous missed opportunity: instead of setting out to discover what people actually wanted from the European Union by engendering a widespread discussion on its aims, objectives, policies and institutions, an attempt was made to bludgeon the people into approving it on the basis that it was acceptable to 'those in the know'. Instead of increasing popular awareness and understanding of the European idea, stimulating fresh ideas and engendering a new enthusiasm, it had the effect of encouraging at best scepticism and, at worst, hostility even among many who had previously been sympathetic.

Above all, it showed up the enormous gap between the political and economic elites and ordinary people. This was exacerbated by an inherent contradiction in the way the constitution was explained: one the one hand, it was sold as a new vision for the Union and, on the other, as merely the simplification and rationalisation of existing treaties. In the event, it fell between two stools and its opponents were provided with all the weapons they could need to attack it. Although its style was much simpler and clearer than many opponents suggested, it smacked of an incomplete and uneasy compromise not only between federalism and inter-governmentalism but also between differing economic philosophies and between those wishing to see Europe exercise unified leadership in the world and those still under the illusion that foreign policy could best be exercised at a national level. It was all too easy to unpick the different strands and reduce the garment to a pile of unwoven threads.

The worst decision now would be to simply return to those who have rejected it in the forlorn hope they may change their minds. Europe does need a constitution but before such a document is acceptable to its citizens, I believe that the European Union must engage in two vital but separate tasks.

Its successor – the Lisbon treaty – has lost its constitutional ambitions and will be ratified, without much enthusiasm, as a practical way forward for structures that were designed for 15 but now have to cope with 27 member states. The time has come for those who understand the vision to regain the initiative and, if it is to succeed in doing so, the European Union must engage in two vital but separate tasks.

First, and obviously working through the offices of the member states, it must begin to ask its citizens what kind of European Union they want. This must not be some cursory consultation designed to camouflage decisions already made but a genuine outreach to grassroots opinion in all the member states. Nor should it be conducted in the media alone but resources should be made available to encourage the participation of the widest range of civil society from local communities to academics, from trades unions and business to faith groups and not forgetting schools and colleges, from which the next generation of ideas can be gleaned. This does not imply a renegotiation of the treaties – that would be patently absurd – but it would allow for sensitive amendment, where necessary, and the incorporation into a final constitutional draft of those new ideas that carry widespread support and the elimination of those aspects of existing legislation revealed as widely unpopular. Above all, it would place a requirement on member states' governments to explain to their electorates the reasoning behind decisions that may be locally unpopular or misunderstood.

This may well be a burden few governments wish to shoulder but that is part of the problem: for far too long, the institutions of the Union have been used as a scapegoat for decisions for which governments evaded responsibility. Important contradictions have been fudged, sometimes for good reason, but more often because a lack of clarity allowed loopholes to be exploited. Genuine and widespread consultation will also serve to reveal underlying values and determine whether the European Union should be reinforcing the social solidarity model of taxation and welfare or seeking to adopt a more transatlantic neo-liberalism – issues which served to blur analysis of the results of the referenda.

The second, very different, but equally important task, is for the European Union to decide if and how it is to exercise leadership in issues of global concern, most especially poverty, human security and climate change. There is a growing need for a united European input in world affairs that promotes an integrationist, rational and multi-lateral approach to international relations. The European experience of pooling national sovereignty should offer immense insights into the underlying causes of conflict in other regions. Its success in turning historically ambitious and aggressive states into cooperative partners prepared to accept the rule of international law should be promoted as a beacon of hope in a world that has to unite if it is not to destroy itself by a failure to confront problems that pose a terminal threat. And time is not on our side. The threat posed by climate change to the very survival of the human species is real and Europe does not have the luxury of time to sort out its own internal problems before engaging with the rest of the world in the attempt to find a solution. It must not allow its energy to be sapped by concentrating only on its internal problems, it must have the courage to play its full part in world affairs.

Most specifically, Europe should begin to look outwards towards the developing nations of the global south in order to explore ways in which its experience of shared institutions might be used to build a coalition of nations capable of tackling the immense dangers of climate change. The lesson of Europe is that good intentions are not sufficient to bring lasting change. Peace, prosperity and justice require institutions and the rule of law. And Europe's unique experience in creating workable institutions must now be used to forge new relationships in the wider world.

Karlheinz Stockhausen (1928-2007)
Composer
www.stockhausen.org

We are rehearsing daily for concerts and running courses with up to nine performances in August, and there are 72 seminars given by interpreters and musicologists for 140 participants from 25 countries, all for the Stockhausen Courses Kürten (which have been held annually for the past seven years). In addition to six world premières we will rehearse for 43 days following the courses for a world première at the Donaueschingen Music Days. Then there will be three concerts in Berlin, nine in Italy, etc etc.

The best musicians who perform with me are not all Germans. In the new work for Donaueschingen, two of the soloists are Dutch, one is German, one is Spanish, and one is American. For years, 35 percent has been automatically deducted from the fees of all non-German musicians for "foreigners' tax". This nasty treatment is only one minor example of the state practice of exploiting artistic quality. Of course we Germans receive the same unjust treatment in France, Italy, Holland, etc. Yesterday, I had to pay 68 EUR plus 20 EUR for bank charges to cash a 19 EUR cheque issued in France.

Europe is in the newspapers and is being defeated by the tax authorities in the banks – and ABROAD.

Something must be done to restore "sufficient respect for the rights of the individual."

Alan Sked

Reader in International History at LSE, founder and first leader of the UK Independence Party (left 1997)

Memoirs of a Eurosceptic

It seems a long time ago now, but as an idealistic teenager in Scotland I joined Jo Grimond's Liberal party. That man had charisma and integrity on a huge scale and he matched both with intelligence. One of the great days of my life was introducing him at Glasgow University when I became president of the university Liberal club there. I also became president of the Association of Scottish Liberal Students, treasurer of the Scottish League of Young Liberals and finally, after I had moved on to Oxford to read for my D.Phil., a Liberal parliamentary candidate in Paisley. (I lost my first deposit there.)

I remained a Liberal at Oxford (something my supervisor, AJP Taylor, tolerated or ignored) and even after I joined the international history department at the LSE, I voted for staying in the EEC in the 1975 referendum and was still a strong federalist supporting a policy of a "federal Britain in a federal Europe", Liberal-style, into the 1980s. But by the end of that decade I had abandoned my support for the EU.

The main reason for becoming a Eurosceptic was that from 1980 to 1990 I served as Convenor of European Studies at the LSE. In other words, I coordinated the interdisciplinary MSc programme on contemporary Europe. In fact, I built it up to be the biggest of any such postgraduate programme in the UK. But in so doing, I had to chair or attend seminar after European research seminar, mark exams, read dissertations, meet Eurocrats and Europhiles galore, until reality eventually broke in. The whole system, I concluded, was unnecessary and mad. The final realisation came after a seminar talk given by the fattest man in the world, who also happened to be the Brussels bureaucrat in charge of transport for the EU. He verily bounced along with a pointer in front of several maps, shouting "I say NO!" And what he was saying no to were the transport proposals of a variety of European governments. He would only approve them, he said, if "all roads lead to Brussels". Watching this obese lunatic with his stick, I felt that Europe would be better off without him – and without his colleagues, and their structures, and especially their imperial ambitions.

The 1980s, of course, had also witnessed the growing battle between Mrs Thatcher and Brussels, first over the British budget contribution and later over everything. Jacques Delors' arrogant and unprecedented intervention in UK domestic affairs at the TUC conference in 1987 then led to Mrs Thatcher's Bruges speech, after which a group of academics, including myself, were asked to establish the Bruges Group, to spread Mrs Thatcher's Eurosceptic ideas. I soon became the main pamphleteer and spokesperson for the Group, and wrote a pamphlet on Germany and the Gulf War plus a statement about the Kurds in its aftermath. "Major A Wimp" was the front page headline in the London Evening Standard, quoting my interview on the Today programme. This led to a great deal of noise and controversy. The Bruges Group then had some influence, but I was summarily expelled from it that same year for founding the Anti-Federalist League and announcing my intention to stand at the 1992 general election against the Tory party chairman and leading Europhile, Chris Patten. (Professor Ken Minogue, an LSE colleague no less, told me that I was becoming "an embarrassment to John Major". So I was thrown out of the supposedly non-party group and Minogue tried to tell the membership that I had "retired", something which, since I was present, he had to retract.)

I then managed to kill Patten's parliamentary career in Bath in 1992, not by the number of votes I received but because I got him to confess at the main public meeting of the 1992 election (which got national media coverage) that he would not apologise for the poll tax. The next morning's national and local headline, "Patten refuses to apologise for the poll tax," effectively finished him off. He still, according to the Times and other sources, blames me for the fact that he never became prime minister.

After the 1992 election, I stood in two by-elections in 1993, first at Newbury and then at Christchurch. I came fourth in both, just 500 votes behind Labour. So with a number of staunch supporters I turned the Anti-Federalist League into the UK Independence Party at a meeting at the LSE in October 1993. I led it into the 1994 European elections (during which my appendix had to be removed) and then into the general election of 1997 after which I quit the party.

The eurosceptic vote in 1997, however, was split by the advent of the Referendum Party. This was set up deliberately to squash UKIP and almost did so, since it was fronted by the wealthy Sir James Goldsmith, whose policy during the campaign shifted from one of "we don't care which side of the argument you're on, so long as you back a referendum" to a policy of backing withdrawal. Goldsmith did the Eurosceptic movement a great service, however, by securing a promise from the Tories that they would hold a referendum on the euro, a promise which Blair subsequently backed. He did it less of a service by deluding it that it should rely on millionaires rather than on hard work and organisation to further the cause. In any case, exhausted after the election, confident that Goldsmith would now lead the cause, (I had no idea that he would die within the year), betrayed by a colleague (an ex-PhD student no less) who turned out to be a mole for the BNP, and appalled by the kind of people who now seemed poised to make a takeover bid for UKIP, I decided to quit. I left a note for the party in HQ saying goodbye, appointed an acting leader and took my leave. The best of my colleagues quit with me.

For a year after I left, the party did well. Then a new leader, Michael Holmes, was elected who seemed to promise wealth and success, but who in fact brought in extreme right-wingers, changed the policy about taking up seats in the European parliament, and in 1999 managed to get himself and two others elected as MEPs. This was a disaster. In his maiden speech, Holmes called to federalist applause for increased powers for the European Parliament. His colleague, Nigel Farage, told him "Well done!" But when it was finally established what had happened (the party tried to deny what had been said), Holmes was flung out. Later MEPs have been no better or wiser. They take their inflated salaries and expenses, while denouncing the system they profit from. If the original idea was that UKIP should subvert the European Parliament, the European Parliament has subverted UKIP. The party now focuses its efforts on retaining its MEPs or securing more, while neglecting the opportunity of entering the UK Parliament – the only body empowered to take us out of the EU.

In the meantime, appalled by UKIP stupidity, its obsession with immigration, not to mention its links with the BNP and other extreme right-wing groups, I have advised voters to vote Tory. That party's policy is far from perfect, but it is the only, now avowedly Eurosceptic party, (all my campaigning did help change something!), with a chance of office. And if it attempts to implement its European policies, should it actually achieve office, it will be forced to renegotiate Britain's place in the EU. If it doesn't achieve office, or merely accepts what it is likely to be told by Brussels once it does, well ... one can always start again. One way or another, Britain will leave the EU.

Michael Sandle
Sculptor and Royal Academician

Thoughts About Germany

I used to have a curiosity bordering on fascination about Germany. Perhaps it was because I was born three years before the Second World War. Childhood memories of the war years still seem remarkably fresh even after sixty years. I remember experiencing the bombing of Plymouth as if it was a kind of 'Son et Lumière' spectacle – searchlights, sirens, the strange 'side to side' throbbing sound from the German bombers as they feathered their engines and the surreal musical tinkling of falling masonry. I did not suffer any hardship and never experienced any fear – my mother's panic when she grabbed me and rushed to the shelters didn't rub off – although the bombing got so bad that we had to be evacuated to Cornwall. One day my mother took me to Plymouth by train and pointed out of the window to where we used to live – for an arc of 180 degrees there was just rubble. You never forget sights like that. Eventually you want to know more about the people who were trying to kill you.

Then there were the films; seen a bit later, but still at a very impressionable age. The Germans (and Austrians) were always portrayed as cruel and ruthless but not without a certain charisma and they had glamorous uniforms thanks – according to John Pilger – to a certain Hugo Boss. And then there was the German speaking nation's art, philosophy, literature, science and, above all, music which affected or maybe infected me. All of this had to be squared with an increasing awareness of the scale of the crimes committed by the Nazis. It is as only a small part of that huge mosaic of evil that the father of my first wife Cynthia was a Czechoslovakian Jew whose entire family died in the Holocaust – he was the only one left because he had found his way to New York where he prospered. He developed a classic survivor's guilt which he then took out on his daughter. This made her psychologically ill and she then became dependent on drugs and died in her early forties.

Why then did I decide to move to Germany? I am a sculptor and had exhibited a large glassfibre reinforced polyester sculpture called 'Oranges and Lemons' in the Paris Biennale in 1966, and this was to play a significant part in my ending up in Germany because Dr Arnold Bode, the founder of the major four-yearly survey show of contemporary art, the 'Documenta', saw it in Paris. He arranged that it be shown later in Kassel in (West) Germany in the forthcoming 'Documenta 4' exhibition. My sculpture was subsequently received well enough in Germany for this to become a turning point in my career. The party given by the West German Embassy for all of the participants of the 1966 Paris Biennale also influenced my decision; I remember that everyone was made welcome, including four or five of my friends and also my mother, who insisted on coming along. This contrasted sharply with the British effort the evening before – only the British contingent was invited and the fare was pretty meagre – some bowls of peanuts and small glasses of dry Sherry to be consumed in an atmosphere of tongue-tied small-talk. The West Germans held theirs in a huge salon which had sideboards groaning under the weight of more food than I had ever seen in my life; someone in tails was playing a white grand piano, the place was awash with pink champagne and full of glamorous men and women in evening dress. I remember the film star Kurt Jurgens bowing and gallantly kissing my mother's hand. Superficial all of this may well be – but it did go through my mind: if this is how they treat artists in Germany then maybe I should go there.

Because of my success at showing at Documenta, I was offered a position as a *gastdozent* (guest lecturer) at the Fachhochschule für Gestaltung, (equivalent to a Technical High School), in the town of Pforzheim, centre of the German Watchmaking and Jewellery Industry, to teach sculpture to design students. I turned the job down (in a letter which was misunderstood because I wrote it in such polite English) because I wanted to go to Berlin. Only through a chance encounter with a German acquaintance in Baden-Baden did I learn that I had got the job, partially due to his efforts, and that the staff at the school were very much hoping that I would turn up, although not really believing that I would. When I eventually turned up at the Fachhochschule in Pforzheim, I was extremely touched to find the staff so obviously pleased to see me. They could not have been more welcoming. I was shown the studio, or 'Dienstatelier', that would be mine by the then Rektor of the school – Professor Eckhart Mosny. It was a huge room that impressed me by its untidiness – as in fact did the whole place. It was all scruffy, there were curtains that were not much better than rags. Not at all what I had expected of Germany. However the Jugendstil building with large studio windows was not without charm. It was one of the few buildings left standing after the RAF had flattened Pforzheim a few weeks before the end of the war.

"This is your studio," Professor Mosny told me, "you can work in it day and night. You only have to teach sculpture to the students two days a week – the rest of the time is yours to do your own work."

I took the job and as it happened, I was also able to spend some time in Berlin. I couldn't speak any German then but I soon got a useable patois going by reading Axel Springer's *Bild Zeitung* – a populist rag certainly but a treatise on hermeneutics compared with *The Sun*. Admittedly the *Bild Zeitung's* headlines are spectacularly lurid but this meant I was very keen to find out their meaning – thirty years later I can still remember many of them. I just *had* to translate them in order to uncover gems like 'Girl Raped in a Wardrobe by German Tenor' or 'Queen Mother has a Colostomy' or 'One Million Hiccups – He Jumped to His Death' or 'Mother of Two Eaten by a Polar Bear' or, how about, 'Unwitting (ahnungslos) Porno Girl Beheaded in Front of the Camera'? However, what seriously impressed me later on was to discover that, contrary to the received propaganda, Axel Springer was *not* a total reactionary– he actually ran a campaign against capital punishment in this paper. He quoted many instances of people being guillotined in Nazi Germany for committing trivial offences like stealing a bar of chocolate.

A few years into the Pforzheim period, I had DAAD stipendium which enabled me to spend half of every week in West Berlin. This was a remarkable place during the Cold War – the underground and overground systems (S Bahn) went through but did not stop at stations in East Berlin and were deserted except for steel helmeted soldiers carrying weapons. At this time I couldn't be bothered with the intimidating business of getting through Checkpoint Charlie in order to visit the East Sector. A few years later, however, I did go through and it was more than worth the effort to marvel at the Schinkel buildings, the Augustus Kiss sculptures and, above all, the stupendous Pergamon Altar.

I stayed for a further five years in Pforzheim and was made a professor before moving a few miles down the road to the Academy of Visual Arts in Karlsruhe. I stayed in Karlsruhe for a further 19 years. The German system of art education is based on the 'Atelier' tradition and this means that any teacher has got to be a practising established artist. This means that very often leading figures in contemporary art become professors, like Joseph Beuys, for example, at the Düsseldorf Academy. When I was at the Academy of Visual Art (Akademie der Bildenden Kunste) in Karlsruhe in the 1980s, Horst Antes, Georg Baselitz, Per Kirkeby and Markus Lüpertz were all teaching there. Unlike Britain, every artist/ teacher is given a proper studio within the academy's premises and is expected to produce work there. Each artist /teacher is allocated his/her own group of students and is solely responsible for their development right up to the 'Meisterschüler' postgraduate stage. The Academy built me a studio complete with a five tonne traversing crane in the grounds of Schloss Scheibenhardt, an 18th Century castle situated in countryside just outside the City and used as studio and classroom accommodation in addition to the Academy's main premises in the centre of Karlsruhe.

Working alone in the grounds at night should have been more creepy than it was. The Gestapo were supposed to have used the place to interrogate prisoners; cadavers were apparently dug up after the war, all with small calibre bullet holes in the back of the heads. I never felt the hairs stand up on the back of my neck, even though I knew that there was a sinister steel panelled room in the basement of the hunting lodge just outside the castle gate. The academy in Karlsruhe has some more skeletons in its cupboards – the Rektor during the war years, Adolf Buhle, had been a rabid Nazi and it was he (not Adolf Ziegler as is often stated) who was responsible for setting up the infamous *Entartete Kunst* (Degenerate Art) Programme. Interestingly enough, had Goebbels, the patron saint of advertising and spin, had his way, the German Expressionists would have represented the Nazis. Not too many people know either that Emil Nolde was the first person to join the Nazi Party – I mean by that, he was a card carrying member and owned Nazi Party Card No.1. He was heartbroken when they threw him out.

As I got to know Germans, I could see that maybe some received notions about them are perhaps justified – they are indeed often inflexible and sometimes frightening – like Professor Von Hagen who seems to be continuing the tradition of making things out of human skin even if they are not lampshades. There is perhaps an occasional 'matter of factness' about sensitive issues that still jars – I remember some years ago being appalled when I read that a Schools Authority somewhere in Germany was thinking of heating an Infants School with hot air channelled from a nearby Crematorium. Not a million miles away from the idea the Nazis had of building the seven huge brick gasometers in Auschwitz (they are still there) to collect the excrement from the prisoners in order to produce methane gas for the Wehrmacht.

Having said all of this, I have to stress that I was always treated incredibly well and by every strand of German society I came into contact with. Even in Pforzheim which we, the British, bombed flat. Even when I couldn't speak a word of their language. It undoubtedly helped that I have blue eyes and look like them – and that my name Sandle sounds almost Swabian because of the way they constantly use 'le' as a diminutive. A Japanese friend who lives in Stuttgart cannot recount quite the same but he would agree there are generous and noble spirits in Germany. I felt privileged to be amongst them. Sometimes I even feel that modern Germany has become a better and fairer society than Britain, although there are worrying signs of unrest. My German friends complain bitterly that the economy is in a terrible mess – well maybe – but you are certainly more likely to be beaten to death in police custody in Britain than in Germany. Having lived in France and Italy as well, I really do believe that Germans have more in common with us than any other Europeans. So much so that the last two wars seem almost like civil wars. It now seems an appalling obscenity that we were killing each other. And Germans do have a sense of humour. But what of their Teutonic efficiency?

I once received a phone call that began “Herr Sandle, here is Oberkomissar Zimmermann from the Criminal Police Department in Karlsruhe“ – in German of course. I felt more than a bit of unease wondering what I had done – had I been caught speeding or something? However, Herr Zimmermann went on to tell me he had on his desk a pile of drawings, letters and other possessions which a student (not one of mine), apparently suffering from some kind personality disorder, had stolen from my studio. I had not noticed that these things were missing. Herr Zimmermann arranged to visit me in order to investigate the break-in. He eventually turned up, friendlier and younger than I had expected, wearing jeans and looking a bit like a cross between Vincent Van Gogh and a hippy. He brought along another young man who wore a sweater and a young policewoman in uniform.

Herr Zimmermann talked incessantly into a hand-held tape recorder, the man in the sweater took endless photographs of the window sill, the supposed point of entry and the policewoman took notes. They were there for ages and I began to get very impatient for them to go. Eventually they did all leave. An hour later a sheepish Herr Zimmermann phoned to say that they would have to do it all over again – there was no film in the camera.

John Martin
Professor of Cardiovascular Medicine, University College London

A European Doctor

The history of the human race is one of change. Not a change of the herd alone, but one in which individuals change in a way that enhances their potential. When we have a choice, it takes courage to choose the path that means giving up something of the past; to take a risk to advance. The concept of the European Union is a social and political advance for man that I believe is a step change on the path of human historical evolution. At a time when politicians are universally self-interested, it has given me a cause which is greater than myself; a cause on the path of human enhancement.

My joy on seeing the EU flag for the first time on the tail of an Air France plane while on a journey to meet my French wife in Paris is long gone. It is now consolidated into a reality. The EU has become part of my life. Young citizens do not remember the Soviet Union and accept that men walked on the moon at some time in past history. In the same way they do not question the movement of labour in Europe; it is part of their lives, it is like having a television and a telephone in a house: "how else could it be?" The European ideal (of which later) is something that helps give reason to my life and the existence of the EU has a very concrete influence on my life. I am a doctor who looks after patients with heart attacks and who does research into why heart attacks occur. I am also a member of the board of the European Society of Cardiology, which is a democratic organisation representing 47,000 heart specialists in Europe. My role within that organisation is to be in charge of the relations of those doctors, as a body, with the institutions of the EU. This role has made me understand that working within a European community has immense advantages for the people of Europe and has benefits that cannot be obtained by working only at the national level. The heart doctors of Europe have set up relationships between themselves which are the living EU. We have demonstrated that it is possible that a professional body, which is pan-european, can analyse a problem of the people (in this case heart disease), create a pan-european plan, whose veracity is determined not by short term political gain of any party or government only interested in the next few years, but a plan that has a professional objectivity, truly directed towards the long term needs of the citizen.

Doctors and scientists worked together to examine the evidence for what might cause death from heart attacks and suffering from heart failure in the European community, by comparing differences in the death rates across Europe, from north to south and from east to west, and relating that to the understanding of the science of how the human heart goes wrong. After much debate, seeing the problem from many different points of view, from different cultures, from different historical perspectives and from different political backgrounds, we wrote a 'Heart Plan for Europe'. Everyone spoke English in the debate. The prevention of heart disease (which kills more citizens of the EU than any other disease) is generally recognised as important across Europe. However, every government has a different approach. That is fine if the approach is tailored to the needs of the people of that country. Often it is not. Making the European population healthier has to be seen as a project with a 20-year vision. The 'Heart Plan' is both simple and deep. The essence is that every European citizen should have the right to have a cholesterol level below five and a blood pressure reading below 140/90. Furthermore, national governments should make every effort to make sure that its citizens do not smoke and that they take exercise. Under this plan Europeans would be healthier and health costs would decrease. The professional cardiology organisations in each country were not strong enough to obtain such an objective or put such a plan into action politically. However, the pan-european organisation had the strength and authority to do that. (This system of action is applicable to other professional bodies representing lawyers, engineers, sociologists and even artists, who could analyse problems from the professional point of view and give solutions to government at the European level).

The presidency of the EU rotates through six-monthly cycles. Upon advice from officials in the European Commission (which has a particular interest in preventing heart disease), we took the plan to the Irish Minister of Health, who saw the logic of working with a large professional organisation. The Irish Government agreed to make the Plan its central objective in health during its presidency. The heart doctors of Europe worked with the Irish Government to modify the Plan so that it was politically acceptable to other European governments, to the European Commission and to the European Parliament. An expert conference was held, whereby the Plan was debated between doctors and politicians and the evidence for the Plan and the means of putting it into action were discussed. This meeting was attended by representatives of the ministries of health of the 25 countries of the EU. A similar meeting was held in the European Commission so that it could see the views of the ministries of health and indicate its agreement or concerns. The Plan was also taken to a small group of members of the European Parliament who were either interested in health, were ex-health ministers of member states or were doctors or nurses. The Irish Government submitted the Plan to a meeting of the Council of Health Ministers of the EU in June 2004. Before this meeting heart doctors from each of the 25 countries of the EU had visited their ministries of health to support the Plan and to explain the reasons why it was important. Thus, when the 25 Ministers of Health met in Brussels, they had been educated by their own doctors concerning the unified message. The Plan was passed unanimously and the European Commission was invited to put the Plan into action across Europe. Not only did the doctors wish to initiate the Plan, but we also wished to help execute it. We have, therefore, worked with the European Commission on the means of implementing the Plan in a partnership between heart doctors and governments. A key to the success of this is to offer a 'tool box', to each country, of ways of achieving low cholesterol and low blood pressure (for example by diet, exercise, public education and appropriate use of drugs), so that under the principles of subsidiarity each country could decide its own ways of achieving the common goal.

In making that choice ministries could see what had been successful in other member states. It was recognised by all concerned that the common goal could be achieved, as a heart attack is a heart attack whether it occurs in Finland or Portugal, in Scotland or Slovakia. It has similar causes and similar consequences in each country.

We are now tackling other problems that can be seen only by professionals from a European perspective. For example, the European Society of Cardiology has concluded that, per head of population, Germany implants twice as many coronary artery stents as the UK. Either one government is wasting money or the other is not giving adequate treatment.

The heart doctors of Europe have shown that Europe can work to the benefit of its citizens. A system of political action has been undertaken that arose from the doctors themselves in a way that was not possible at the national level. The membership of the European Society of Cardiology is by definition drawn from every country of the European Union. However, among its leadership there is a disproportionate number of British doctors. This is not only because of the high regard for British medicine, achievement and organisation in the rest of Europe, but also because native English speakers in Europe have an advantage over others who speak it as a second or third language. It is a tragedy for Britain that our natural leadership position in Europe has not been grasped by successive governments who have lacked the long term vision or courage to see that Britain could have been the major leadership force in Europe over several decades.

A culture of cynicism and 'let's wait and see' has pervaded decisions both from Conservative and Labour governments. In historical hindsight this may well be seen as the consequences of post-imperial self doubt.

"I am not having them telling us what to do," is the most often heard phrase from Euro-sceptics in Britain when talking about the European Commission and the other institutions of the EU. In society everyone has to accept somebody telling them what to do so that society functions, even if it is as simple as driving on the left or right hand side of the road. Of course, there have been some inappropriate decisions made by the European Commission; that is only natural in a large organisation. However, there has been a continuous lack of information in the British press about the benefits that the European Commission has brought to British life, for example cheaper car prices and cleaner beaches. Above I have given an example of how working together can improve the health of European hearts.

I believe that the greatest tragedy for human beings is failure to achieve their full potential due to lack of training, education, understanding or bad luck. Most individuals do not fulfil their human possibilities – intellectually, emotionally, creatively or economically. It is a particular shame when an individual is held back because of their personal history. I believe the same can be true at the level of the nation-state. Many Britons have a nostalgia for a British past and are fearful of a European future. This is holding them back from fulfilling their potential in a greater environment. I love warm beer, Nelson, the Yorkshire moors, my commission in the British army, the dry humour of my father, the mother of Parliaments, British discovery and my Georgian house. But I retain all those and use them as a springboard to achieve expanded fulfilment working across the European Union. I am sure there were similar doubts before the unification of Mercia and Northumbria in the 9th century.

A balance must be achieved by politicians between a concept of a united Europe acting together in relation to the outside world (militarily, economically, politically) and the need for individual, particularly regional, identity. I think this has been achieved in Spain, where power has been devolved from central government in Madrid to autonomous regions which can raise local taxes and, for example, decide their own local health care system. Local government ensures that local traditions, cultures and languages are priorities. In fact, in Catalunya one can now sometimes see two flags flying side by side: the flag of Catalunya and the flag of the EU. The natural extension of this is a model of Europe as a collection of two or three hundred autonomous regions, led by a strong central organisation in Brussels that cares for the collective needs of the regions. However, even if this were achievable, it would take a hundred years.

There are often complaints that the idea of what Europe is about is not written down. Here, from my perspective, is the European ideal:

1) A democratic, socialist organisation which is funded by capitalism.
2) Respect for the individual in an environment where it is believed that the individual causes society not that society causes the individual. Individual rights of freedom are seen as qualities without which a good society cannot exist. One manifestation of this is that the death penalty is not used in the EU. (Compare this to the attitude of the United States and China.)
3) A belief that the inner man in the human being has a value greater than money. This inner man is enhanced by education, art, music, philosophy, literature and good health. These are funded by a combination of the state using taxes generated through capitalism and private venture.
4) An understanding that science is the basis of advance in the physical world and that this requires investment and research, that the best ideas are generated in institutions where there is diversity of membership.
5) A belief that these concepts apply to all human beings and can be exported. However, not by military power but by soft empire.
6) A conclusion that in global economics, the EU has the size to protect member states from victimisation.
7) A knowledge that in the future Europe's main export, in exchange for Chinese and Indian goods, will be ideas. Quality of idea is improved by mixing cultures and traditions. Europe has sufficient closeness and sufficient diversity to create leaps of originality.

These ideals, mixed with diverse cultures that understand each other through their shared history and common romano-christian traditions will, I hope, produce a new society that will advance humanity. This advance will be not so much economic as moral, where moral means all those qualities of man that economics support. This concept is, of course, idealistic, but every advance of man has been based upon an idea. There are also pragmatic reasons why member states should work together pooling their sovereignty. There is better action against crime, illegal immigration and terrorism. Defence and foreign policies can be strengthened. Environmental problems can be tackled together. Research in all areas is strengthened and trade policy negotiations are easier at the European level. My real reason for believing in Europe, however, is the idealistic one.

One unresolved problem is the final size of the European Union. Is it to be an organisation, be it federalist or a group of nation-states, that spreads itself wider and wider to those willing to accept its principles? Or is it to reach a defined limit based upon a principle? There are pragmatic reasons why the second approach is better. This is not because human organisations in history that have become wider and wider have always collapsed but because the belief that the concept of the European Ideal (outlined above) arises from the Christian inheritance of Europe. Even though most of us do not go to church, indeed have an ambiguity about belief in god, it is important to recognise that the evolution of the European Ideal has occurred through a Christian intellectual tradition. Our laws, social behaviour, economic rules, military behaviour are all based upon a Christian tradition. In the future there will be times of difficulty within the EU and at those times we will naturally regress to our Christian roots for a solution. As Freud recognised we cannot do otherwise. That is the nature of human behaviour.

This, however, raises the problem of whether a large Muslim country should join the EU. I love travelling in Turkey. One of my greatest delights is to sit by the Bosphorus watching ships go up and down drinking Turkish coffee. The Turkish tradition is Islamic, now of course manifesting itself in a secular state. That state may well not differ from other members of the EU in times of plenty. However, when there are difficulties I believe that a state of Islamic tradition may revert to its earlier traditions. For example, inherent in European political development over the last 1,000 years has been the separation of church and state: "Give unto Caesar what is Caesar's and unto God what is God's." Islam itself does not recognise such a separation, nor has it gone through a renaissance. Although Ataturk determined that there was a separation of church and state in modern Turkey, this concept of a secular state may have been made possible by the will and power of the army. Under the ethical rules of the EU the Turkish army's influence will no longer be possible. Unfortunately, we cannot run a scientific experiment to see how Turkey would behave without the army when, for example, imams do not have to submit their sermons every week for approval. They may not encourage radical Islam, but I believe there is a danger that they may in times of crisis. Some would argue that if Turkey does not enter the EU it might become a fundamentalist Islamic state. That may be so, but the greater danger is that it enters the EU as the largest country and then becomes a radical Islamic state. Neither the European Union, nor Turkey has to take the risk. I love Turkey because it is Eastern. Some of its more potent symbols are the large black Islamic plaques that cover the golden Byzantine mosaics in the church of Santa Sofia on the European side of the Bosphorus.

I recently returned from a visit to China as part of a European Commission delegation on science and technology. The economic advances were extraordinary. However, Chinese government ministers said that China could no longer rely upon bringing in resources from the rest of the world. Its objective was to increase the living standards of its people and this could only be achieved by using its greatest natural resource, its people. To do this Chinese innovation was needed. The government looked to Europe which it said, repeatedly, was "a great civilisation", like Chinese civilisation. It became clear to me that in the future the important business will be done between great blocks. Britain alone would have a poorer relationship with China if it were not part of the EU. Furthermore as future larger economic blocks emerge in the world (for example China, India, Brazil and Japan have been suggested) the EU will assume greater importance for Britain.

But my main reason for believing in the EU is not negative but positive. Human beings need a vision, a destiny that looks further than the effects of marketing on their consumer behaviour. I look forward to a new society, built upon the European tradition that values personal internal development more than economic gain, while at the same time recognising that economics are essential for each individual's success.

These are my personal views and do not necessarily reflect the views of the European Society of Cardiology or University College London.

Stephen Woolley

Film-maker, producer of numerous films including Company of Wolves, Scandal, Mona Lisa, Interview with a Vampire, End of the Affair, The Crying Game, *and director of* Stoned

In the past few years of producing and directing movies in Europe, I've been fortunate enough to have fostered an incredible bond with fellow filmmakers across the continent. The visual art removes barriers and more and more funding and tax incentives are to be found from Dublin to Denmark. Sadly, an upward trend in European co-productions is matched by a downward trend in European distribution companies' hunger for European product. This is vividly illustrated by a conversation which took place a few years ago between myself and a major French independent distributor in Cannes. Whilst pitching a project the distributor stopped me midflow and looked seriously into my eyes, held my script aloft and exclaimed, "I don't have to read this, I know if you're this passionate it's going to be good. I trust you to deliver a good movie and your cast is terrific. So I'm in, on one condition: you guarantee a US release. Tell me you have US distribution and we are on board." I didn't, so he wasn't.

So as long as we make European cinema that is acceptable to the US then itwill be acceptable to Europe. This bizarre filtration process sadly has some basis in reality. In 1993, I financed *The Crying Game* with no US money but crucial contributions from French, Italian, German and Spanish sources. The film was successfully released in the US after its completion and received a handful of Oscar nominations.

It was distributed in France and Germany before the US and performed poorly. In Spain, Italy and Scandinavia it was a smash hit riding on the coat tails of its US box office performance. The situation is exacerbated by the media's obsession with perceived success. As the internet, DVD and satellite draw the world closer, the desire for instant hit or flop becomes paramount. And the label sticks.

It's common knowledge that US films are generally out grossing home product with a few notable exceptions. What's disappointing is that, whilst there is a great deal of incentive to produce films in a European context, only those filmmakers with a record of success in the States can easily find the backing from the essential distribution and sales arms that exist here. Many films can raise up to 60 percent of their budgets through production, tax and incentive funds – shooting a UK/Irish co-production gives access to these funds and we share a common language with North America. Even so, an end user must be involved to square the circle, and often they will only take a risk with tried and tested talents or genre (comedy, horror, thriller) and the larger budget movies are taking advantage of the incentives. 'British' movies made recently include *Resident Evil: Apocalypse*, *Alien Vs Predator*, *Alexander* and *Sahara*. Made by Sony, Fox, Warner Bros and UIP respectively.

It's true that we must attract Hollywood money to Europe but we must also find a way to make more original, indigenous and ground-breaking European movies. That can only happen if European distribution is willing to take a risk with first time directors and non-Hollywood subject matter.

Michael Howard
Former leader of the Conservative Party

The last century taught us that when Britain turns her back on Europe, the consequences can be catastrophic. We must not forget that lesson. There is a growing and dangerous rivalry between Europe and America. It is a rivalry that Britain is best placed to stop – and best placed to do so from within the European Union.

In Britain, politicians of all persuasions have made mistakes in their dealings with the European Union. It has not been part of a deliberate deceit, as some people claim, but because we failed to grasp the extent of other countries' ambitions. We believed that talk of political union was mere empty rhetoric. That failure ensured that Britain's relationship with the European Union developed into an institutionalised tug of war – a tug of war which has been as frustrating for us as it has been for our European partners.

The European Constitution will lead to further centralisation and more bureaucracy. It is based on the mistaken belief that it is possible to prescribe in great detail exactly how things should be run, with rights prescribed way beyond those that are the basis of liberal society, such as free speech and free assembly.

We in Europe, so keen to lecture others around the world about human rights and democracy, have produced something that will be remembered by history as a grim, incomprehensible document – a treasure trove for lawyers and an obstacle to free enterprise.

So does this all mean that the European Union is condemned to failure? I do not believe it does. With fundamental reform we can make the European Union work for the benefit of its peoples.

Experience tells us that there are powers which are currently held by the European Union which would be better exercised by national governments. Nation states should be able to take those powers back if they want to. I certainly would want to see powers returned from Brussels to Britain. Allowing countries to pursue their own policies would force the European Union to become more competitive – benefiting us all.

Of course, there are some powers that all countries must sign up to – the single market being the most obvious. The single market was intended by Britain to be a vehicle for liberalisation that would benefit business. It has brought real benefits to countries across Europe – but it has also been used to justify unnecessary rules and regulations. This is partly what has caused the recent steep decline in support for the EU amongst British business.

So we need to look closely at how the single market is working in practice. We need a simple set of rules that will facilitate and stimulate trade within the European Union. A reformed single market must be the bedrock of a transformed EU. It would deliver the great gains in productivity and growth that Europe so desperately needs. It would end the steady creep of bureaucratic power. And it would re-engage public support for the European Union.

Countries which want to pursue 'ever closer union' should be free to do so. But they must accept that others regard this path as a road to nowhere – not the fast lane they perceive it to be. The quid pro quo for allowing them to proceed would be agreement that they cannot force countries which do not wish to join them to do so.

Simon Sykes

Former cultural integration specialist with the Lagardère Groupe and GEC Marconi

Diary extracts during the first Franco-British joint venture between Matra (part of the Lagardère Groupe) and Marconi

February 21, 1990

Squared it with G, [Président Directeur Général] over dinner in Paris; on the back of the integration, the business transformation will ride – he told me about the two shareholders – how they will underpin all efforts to make a success of the venture ... how they intend to expand the business. He confirmed his own commitment as long as, he adds, he has the helm ... bit ominous.

February 22

The UK Exec members obliged me by agreeing to attend pre-programme workshops to establish a clear view of their respective operations; real struggle here, especially from the older British members; they see all this as a waste of time; they believe their tried and tested methods of command and control will prevail over the French if they just stick at it; the younger members defer to the older ones and keep quiet except for a few choice comments designed to enhance their careers ... they'll be lucky – it won't be long before the changing alliances render any notion of personal security void.

February 24

On the face of it, the French members are much more amenable to my suggestions. They have the whip hand and feel duty bound to lead the way – as Europeans, they say. They also like the 'creativity' of it all and already the key differences are becoming apparent to all concerned – neither I nor the French think it odd that I quote from Baudelaire's *Le Voyage* to set the scene for the adventure to come – the Brits however don't register my quote from *Julius Caesar* except by the delivery ... they are all getting frightened at the prospect of having to address this many headed beast of integration / reorganisation. G has produced a statement for the whole workforce to the effect that integration is the number one priority ... it reads like a bizarre version of a wartime Gaullist BBC broadcast – '*les Français parlent aux ... [Anglais]*' (sic).

March 3

Submitted the two workshop agenda (French and British) to G in Paris. He is keen but fears non-cooperation amongst *mes confrères en UK*. We lunch in the site canteen, seen by all. We agreed it will all work out with proper planning ... he laughed and leant across the table to pat my arm. He signed them off with approving nods.

He likes the big picture in all this – especially since it will enable him to re-organise the whole mess he has inherited. Mentioned as an aside that we may be looking at German, Italian and Spanish partners and a further British associate, (he means takeovers) – good grief! A truly European venture to take on the Americans, he enthused. I didn't press him as to who exactly they might be. Anyway I've a fair idea – nightmare.

Ran around the top floor getting available dates from the Exec members – they know I have lunched with G so are very amenable.

Flight back through storm – women weeping as we almost crash land!

March 4

Met with UK Exec – showed agenda; explained basic premise (again). They displayed fear and began arguing over minutiae while masking their genuine apprehensions. Someone tried to rationalise their apprehension through an a-b-c-arian 'treatise' on *The Dambusters* as the epitome of British values – he'd lost his mind and the rest of us lost track; I suggested some individual 'pre-pre' programme meetings which they all agreed to.

March 5/6/7

Met individual UK members to explain exactly what the objectives are – just have to be honest, I tell them – no point in bullshitting. Several visibly went into 'bunker mode' at the prospect of revealing their lost domains to all and sundry.

March 9/10

Paris to meet the French Exec. They exuded confidence over their approaching 'audit' – they say they know their business. This is shaping up for a stand-off based on each side simply reinforcing their own notions of the way forward, no matter how full of holes ... all have strengths ... and weaknesses. I've said often enough that the future lies in maximising the strengths – typically they see their strengths as their weaknesses and vice versa.

April 15

London – hotel with British Exec. Much drinking after dinner and much philosophising about the joint venture – every opinion catered for – but it seems to be a simple case of measuring the odds – get in with the French *or* fail – get in with the French *and* fail. I reminded them they have no choice except to get involved – the French have the major share – but the strength of the joint venture lies in its joint capabilities ... etc. More drinking was the solution apparently – a double tot before the battle. Later, three senior managers (independently) tapped me for information and my opinion. They are the three who find the whole thing the least attractive to them – now they are worrying and scheming instead of getting their heads around the challenges. I told them this much to their dismay – they'd better get organised – never done an integration that didn't eventually lose the deadwood. It was late and I resorted to veiled threats ...

April 17

UK workshop began with individuals giving a short explanation of their perceived operational place in the scheme of things. Because of, and despite, their own (obvious) pre-scheming, this proved very disquieting since the lack of coordinated thinking and practice was absolutely evident. The engineering and production representatives are at loggerheads over exactly what processes they are operating – it became clear that they are running little empires cut off from each other and are oblivious to the general requirements of the company. The functional heads just said 'we told you so', and then got hammered for not organising adequate training / resourcing / financing etc. Blatant obsession with hierarchy which matches the French in substance but not in subtlety.

Depressing lunch accompanied by more arguing over roles and responsibilities.

I got them to suggest ways in which the house can be put in order. Together we resolved to establish a process map along with a jobs' definition exercise. All slightly despondent at the end, but the objective has been reached. Playing the motivational card, I reminded them that if they can achieve some semblance of self-knowledge regarding their part of the business, they won't look quite so stupid when they come to meet the French.

April 20

Began working with the British Exec in planning the process mapping / jobs definition.

I sought out M [managing director UK] and suggested that we might give the UK workforce the opportunity to participate ... he agreed and I suggested the setting up of a Panel of reps chosen for their free-thinking and open-minded approach to the integration – thin on the ground in this here vicinity – to invite constructive suggestions for improvement from the workforce in general and to address the suggestions made. I intend to do exactly the same thing in France, but I didn't tell him.

April 21

Somewhere in the Cher. Typically, the French workshop is held in a very select Chateau venue. My room is huge and reminiscent of a film set for a revolutionary epic. The dinner was long and heavy and the Exec members took it in turns to complain about the wine. I was trapped next to CM, [Head of Marketing] who, despite my protests, concluded that I was simply an '*eminence grise*' and that the integration campaign was simply a smoke screen – he is rather insecure and yet seemed oddly pleased at having erroneously confirmed his own fears.

Anyway, collectively they seem positive about the workshop. They all seem in good spirits, much due to their belief that they are more sophisticated in these matters than the Brits.

Take stock of some key cultural factors:

- no concept of the organic and the mechanistic
- poor language / communication skills and therefore no way in to each other's psyche
- greater pressure on the French to learn English; the upshot is they defensively pretend to know more than they do; (dangerous)
- very poor historical / cultural knowledge on either side
- never had to investigate value systems – these are engineers mostly and seem to think in compartments which they are unable to link – perfect reflection of commercial / working practices
- heavy reliance on stereotyping and prejudice to reach simple conclusions and strategies

The more they learn of all this, the more they will see the mountain to be climbed.

April 22

Workshop began. Only the obviously insecure acting up – a couple suffering from 'fuck you' syndrome. As in the UK, they each set out their stall, cannily demonstrating seamless process cohesion and functional interlocking. This is of course, nonsense. Unprompted, they nevertheless admitted to possible improvements to their systems, mostly involving expensive software applications and more staffing / office space.

At lunch, RV [human resources], drew me aside and intimated that all is not as well as it seems ... he explained some very dire shortcomings in the process and general operations in France. I told him that everyone needed to be honest since when the programme proper takes place, if the Brits get a whiff of dishonesty it will simply reinforce already held negative perceptions.

With the seed planted we resumed. I resorted to producing some pretty awful figures relating to performance and sales which I asked them to comment on. As one, they became defensive and then began blaming one another. The transformation from the morning's confident cohesion to outright hostility is a sight to behold. I suggested they work on this with some urgency – perhaps process mapping, jobs definition. Panel to involve workforce? In fact they are doing this in the UK – might be worth getting in touch ...? Want some names ...?

Truly in the same boat, but have failed to recognise the fact. I closed by explaining that the approach is one of creating a completely new culture – not the rehashing of the existing – yet necessarily derived from the existing.

April 23

Briefing to G at HQ. He laughs a little insanely when I tell him the Exec have more in common than we thought – meaning poor management and mediocrity in general. He muses that we will have to turn the whole world upside down to achieve this whole integration thing. The scale of the project is coming home to him. I remind him of our conversation a year ago that the whole objective is to improve the way we do business given the changed commercial climate. Cultural Integration is an all-encompassing vehicle, he repeats for our mutual benefit and then asks me about the 'blockers and obstacles' – I maintain it is all about his managers. He is quick to suggest a cull – get a list up. I suggest we wait for the jobs' definition to be completed since this will give us the necessary info. He says he wants to have a Company wide survey done and suggests I talk to someone at COFREMCA – will cost a fortune.

Settle some other stuff before he asked me about my time in Quercy – he's a simple artisan at heart and that's why I like him.

May 15

DC [Ops Director] took me through the process mapping results. They show catastrophic short-circuits; if we were making even something simple it would be disastrous – but the fact that we are producing complicated electronic kit...!

This revelation is reinforced by the massive amount of (often anonymous) info we have received via the Panel from the general workforce. Other than reiterating the operating shortfalls, some of this info has thrown up quite serious allegations of dishonesty and bullying by senior execs – one particularly about bullying by the Manufacturing Director UK which has caused loss of sleep and time off work etc – don't know about validity but handy ammo for my purposes – will have to investigate further.

May 20

More Panel stuff. Anonymous offering setting out some problems regarding the fact that a Frenchman is now in charge of the British Radar sensing division. The implication is that this character will give away lots of secrets to the French military and so to the detriment of British security – all a bit dramatic. Researched further and found that the French have expertise in Optics but not in Radar – Optics are no good if the ground is obscured. Playing it safe, I flagged it to R [MOD]. He called back and seemed quite agitated. Spent the next three hours explaining the whole situation to him. As an outsider, he frightened the both of us at the official ignorance as to the existence of the joint venture and at the possibilities for absolute chaos.

May 30

Endless meetings getting the mapping done. The jobs' definition UK / France is a nightmare confirmed; in plenty of areas, the stated commercial needs of the company bear no relationship to the employees employed and the skills (un)available. This is a gross management deficiency which in the cost-plus days mattered little. In this scenario, G's mission statement is so much tosh.

To compound all this, the French earn between 5 and 15 percent more than the Brits for doing the same job ... their subsidiary get lots more state subsidy – this will only further annoy the Brits.

June 12

Much consternation regarding the 'organigramme' G wants to put out. He quite aggressively justifies his plans regarding some very dodgy re-shuffling. I suggested we will have to become more tyrannical for this to work. He said, "beyond using my charm, I should bang heads together." I replied that it will be counter-productive and suggested, perhaps too seriously, that it would be easier to sack them all and start again. It all got a bit heated but he agreed to hold off until after the holidays. He is understandably getting impatient – for every report I give him, he gets twenty others which are different – regardless of the fact he trusts me, he has to listen and consider other informants – some of whom he has known far longer than me.

June 13

Late arrival at the Chambres de Commerce colloquium. Got into my stride on the organic nature of true cultural integration being so complex that the mechanistic takes over – the systems are simple to construct and only require the people being told what to do ... the organic is thus subsumed leaving only a residue of disaffection to come back and bite you on the arse constantly, etc etc. Audiences always nod sagely at this. The Q&A produces the usual predominance of statements regarding strategies to short-circuit having to deal with people and all their frailties – mechanistic over organic. No questions – all are frightened of having no answers. QED.

June 14/15

Visited all five sites UK / France – palpably poor morale everywhere – general despondency even at high level. Most people simply want to know what is happening.

Inundated with requests for info high and low. Some satisfaction in some quarters at the lack of progress. Meet G – he too is despondent and holds no punches in blaming the Brits for dragging down the French – he's all *où sont les neiges d'antan?*

Bad sign. Mad taxi drive to airport – just get plane after much argument with officious staff.

Met with MOD rep. on arrival in UK. He informed me that this Optics / Radar thing has gone to the highest level – mostly because no-one at Government level is the remotest bit aware of what the joint-venture as a whole actually means, let alone any military / security issues. In the lounge, he sat opposite me, eyes wide, arms outstretched and said; "How can two entrepreneurs simply decide to do this without so much as a by your leave?" The way it is.

Note:

After some five difficult years of re-organisation, re-engineering and commercial expansion, some semblance of cultural integration had taken place. A key feature of this was a constantly changing cast of senior executives (as coined; a cast in order of disappearance).

Inevitably and with time, the ever-changing commercial, political and economic situation rendered most of the progress made, irrelevant.

Gareth Rees

Writer

Lawyers and regulators have a *lebensraum* problem, I reckon. They need more space and so they jump on the European free trade project and create an ever-expanding EU thing. But these Leviticus louts are sewing me up with their rules in my place of work and even in my home.

I also work as a cleaner aboard Her Majesty's shore-based ship HMS Nelson. Very soon it will be the bicentenary of the Battle of Trafalgar, a battle which scuppered, for a while at least, the threat of Britain's subjugation to mainland Europe. Thank you Horatio Nelson. And yet, I'm wondering whether his sacrifice was all in vain.

My cleaning job means I go into a fuckload of rooms every day. It gets quite tiring just opening doors without even thinking about the rooms within and the cleaning to be done. Today though, for a while, this door-opening weariness was strangely absent. And then I worked out why this was so. Along this particular corridor, I noticed that when I opened the doors, they opened with minimal effort and, even more liberating, they stayed open so that it was easy for me to drag through my vacuum cleaner.

My pleasure, however, was short-lived. I noticed in the corridor a package outside every door. When I examined one of the packages, I saw that it contained a mechanism which, when attached the door, would require quite a push to open that door and then, if you were hauling a vacuum cleaner, you'd have to lean quite strongly against the door because its desire was to automatically close with a squeaking and then a bang. Bad for the nerves and a drain on a cleaner's precious energy.

Well, it's all about fire safety of course, and who can be against fire safety? But, at the same time, I don't like closed doors. I'm not a fucking prisoner. Who likes to be behind closed doors? People who conspire against the people. Gangsters. Politicians. Perverts.

It would all be all right if I could just go home to my cave. But even into that, the bureaucratic, paternalistic fascism has crept. You have to push so hard to get through the door to my apartment building, you'd almost swear someone was behind that door trying to keep you out. What a welcome home feeling!

And yes, even in my flat the doors are 'fire regulation' ones. I got so maddened being cooped, I copped and tried to hack off the mechanism at the top of one of the doors. But these things are of course policed. I answered my door one day and it was our maintenance man in the company of the fire regulation man. The mechanism I'd hacked at was dangling and I was made to feel guilty of criminal damage as well as being in breach of some EU Directive. The mechanism cost £28 by the way and so the manufacturers' lavish lunch and more beside somewhere in Brussels had been paid for. But that's cynical and my dad used to tell me there's no consolation in this life for cynics.

But is it really the EU's fault for these doors designed to snap off the fingers of infants and those not too sober? Maybe it's a local or national government thing.

Well, along with the top-of-the-door mechanisms came these incredibly sticky posters with little men running on a green background. An arrow indicates where I should run in the event of a fire. I really didn't need to be told the direction of my only exit so I pulled with great effort these posters down and, after one very adhesive job, I fell over backwards and banged my nut.

These posters – I've seen identical ones in Dublin and the same in Prague and Chemnitz. It's got to be an EU thing hasn't it? But government, very, very detailed government just gets so remote you can't be sure where to hang responsibility.

Going back to my dad again, I remember him telling me about a pipe Moses used to play to alleviate the solitude when he was a shepherd. After he died, the pipe was overlaid by craftsmen. It was beautified but there was so much overlay the pipe could play no tune. I reckon all these regulations are sometimes too much overlay that can stifle to death. Lives may be saved from fire but how many cleaners throughout the EU, upon pushing open the hundredth door, find it's one effort too many and keel over with mortal apoplexy?

Jean-Jacques Burnel

Musician with The Stranglers

I was born in London of Norman parents. As a kid growing up in England in the 1950s, I was well aware of the difference between what I was perceived as and how my fellow pupils were perceived. I was a frog and we had had a 'bad' war and my schoolmates' dads had won the war. Later on at secondary school, I joined the Combined Cadet Force and for a short time contemplated going for a commission. However, I was soon put in my place when it was pointed out that, although I had a British passport, I had no chance of a commission since my parents were French. Things have changed since then.

At the time I found it grossly unfair since, by then, I considered myself British with a French background. My schooling was entirely English, historical references almost entirely British and, in fact, all my papers and documents were in the name of John Burnel (despite the name on the passport being Jean-Jacques). I wasn't allowed to be part of what I considered myself to be a part of.

Things have changed immensely since that time. Partly due to the fact that Europe is no longer seen as a faraway place of which we know little, due in part to the evolution that has come about in European institutions: the Common Market, EEC, now EU. The fact of labour movement within EU countries, the fact of stability with war becoming a thing of the past within EU countries, the fact of economic well-being, have all led to tangible benefits for all the citizens of the EU. We in Britain are more cosmopolitan, less provincial now.

Since my late teens I have actually considered myself a European. Twenty five years ago I was almost a European zealot. I even recorded an album called *Euroman Cometh*. I thought that the idea of the nation state had outlived its use and that eventually we would all be citizens of a United States of Europe. I don't believe that anymore. I think it might eventually happen but not by coercion. It should happen, if at all, when the majority of its citizens have overcome their ethnic or local particularities. It won't happen while there is widespread cynicism regarding the widespread corruption right up to the institutions that are supposed to manage European affairs. It won't happen while there is a lack of transparency and accountability in the higher echelons of European power. A great idea, a great vision, has been hijacked by bureaucrats and politicians completely out of touch with the people and in the process they are alienating those same people. Slow down and let people catch up. At least those who care.

Some ideas catch the imagination of all free thinkers. Peace, economic union, freedom of movement, universal suffrage, freedom of thought and expression. Not a premature ejaculation of a European constitution.

Bill Griffiths (1948-2007)
North-East poet

A Voyage to Lupalok

What with the expanding Common Market and the welcome practice of cheap air fares, it was surprising I waited as long as I did before taking advantage and visiting some of those smaller Eastern capitals that had escaped the scourge of war and post-war regeneration.

"No," I explained to the tour operator, "I did not in the least mind encountering a peasant economy; no spoiled plazas with piped pop please."

The lady at the desk smiled tolerantly, did some adjustments to the computer, looked apprehensive for a moment, then recommended Lupalok. "I cannot seem to raise the photo page currently – but look," and she turned the monitor to my view, "this is what it says..."

Lupalok – the smallest capital city in Europa[?] Lovely welcome, pleasant stays and historic city centre, all the way since Price [they meant Prince] Fristobox crossed the Dubo [a river?]. Princes [prices?] for all pockets.

"Charming," I commented. "What is the exchange rate?"

I booked, took advantage of a special offer, and persuaded my step-daughter and her partner to join me; he rather looked as though he expected free vodka as a reward. Perhaps there would be. Yet no more than any of the other explorers (local astronauts us, I thought), did I know what to expect. Some pleasant hotels? A scenic city, with river, castle, medieval streets? Quaint sports and traditions? I sighed.

Doubtless it was all sanitised and organised, in the good name of tourism, even in this nook of nowhere-Europe.

The hotel turned out a group of modern-looking chalets, outside the town, and pleasantly grassed and trimmed. There was a shower (water brackish and even rusty but hot) and a shop, and a separate dining hall, all in the modern mode. Perhaps I should have been prepared for this – but I could not help showing my disappointment.

"I'm sure the centre will be lovely!" said Jenny, to cheer me up, and checked the transport. That first day, we set off together, determined to discover something strange and beautiful, and spend some currency.

'Lupalok' sounds basically cute and predictable, does it not? We were not prepared. The taxi stopped in a street lined with tall buildings, and decorated – though not strictly blocked – with some roaming cattle. From here we must go on foot. We had not far to go. The city of Lupalok turned out to be one rectangle of roads or rather gaps, with tall wooden buildings on all sides and in the middle. It was completely enclosed and claustrophobic, with no vistas or parks, indeed no space to spare for trees or verges. And as we learnt later, no street lighting. In accordance with ancient tradition, the householders left their shutters open, and the light of downstairs windows served to illuminate the cobble roadway.

"Why, it's lovely," said Jenny, rather to my surprise; "medieval?"

One or two buildings had modern-style fronts, but I suspected they were just that – fronts. Otherwise, it did indeed seem unchanged since the time Prince Fristobox first pitched his tent here (as I picture it). Yet the architecture was by no means primitive: the houses extended upward to six or, in some cases, eight floors – a mastery of the wooden skyscraper technique that suggested no very early date. Yet the woodwork itself was utterly plain, relived only by oddly wide flattened windows. Late medieval, I hinted – but if the 'Middle Ages' here had nothing modern to follow it, the term in itself was meaningless.

There were no obvious churches or museums, no stone portals to indicate the public buildings. After walking round the four corners and returning to our start, we decided that buildings with their main doors opened wide, were open to the public; shut, private. We let young Joe pick a hostelry: wisely he went for something quiet, not too crowded, but cheerful looking in its way. I wondered if they would cope with English.

They did, but the hospitality proved to be a choice between bottled beers and casks of the local wine. We chose variously, and settled down to relax at our knotted wooden table, with its irregular shape, and stern but cushioned chairs. There was, I noted with relief, in our wooden context, no fireplace. It seemed this could be why the buildings were so densely built (and densely occupied) – they kept each other warm.

"What," I asked, "happened in the winter?"

The River Dubo, I was assured, due to some underground anomaly, flowed hot at this point, and so moderated the climate of the city, a fire was scarcely needed. We never saw a fire in our stay in Lupalok.

Conversation was polite and friendly, but not forced on us. Only one or two in the whole room knew anything of English. We did learn, however, that the best way to view the city would be to knock two doors along where lived the local guide, who could show us the interiors of notable buildings, etc.

This requires a new section, for if the dull, slightly plum-coloured weather-boarding of Lupalok City was a surprise, the interiors of these dour tenements were a revelation. Culture, in the sense of fine art, may have passed Lupalok by; but folk art was in the greatest abundance, and hardly a square foot of bare inside wood was not carved; not a corner of plastered space left undecorated. With the simplest techniques. The carving was inline and outline, with no rounding or depth; the themes were stylised – explained as people, especially children, and the occasional animal. Likewise the paintings. Soot gave a black pigment for outline. There was a light wash (not fresco I think) in pale green or pale orange (but seldom both). The effect was not unlike naïve painting anywhere else in mainland Europe (or the first attempts at prints in Japan), but the more impressive here because of the plain, barn-like style of the exteriors; and the excellent state of preservation.

Having spent a pleasant morning, clambering and admiring, Jenny and Joe retired to a hostelry; I asked to be taken on to what served as a local 'museum'. This was not in the main nexus but a little beyond, in a low-rise building that looked like a former shed or storehouse. It was in conventional wood but sufficiently modernised to have white plastered walls and electric light. There was no display as such. The curator was busy treating a concreted nodule of some sort of metal. She spoke very good English!

So much of central and eastern Europe, she explained, was destabilised by the Turks, and I must not expect a developed and sophisticated culture in the western sense. When the grip of the Turk relaxed in the 17th century, the people of Lupalok had had to more or less find their own ways of building and belief – not exactly Christian, not exactly Islamic, but entirely peasant. The whole economy was agricultural – wheat, vines and cattle. But so poor, and so poorly organised, that no baron class had emerged to build stone castles or patronise grand art. The folk art I had been introduced to was typical of this – figurative, so not Islamic in origin, but highly stylised, and not touched by western realism or perspective – more like a memory of ancient icon painting. So that "the relative sizes," she went on, "can be deceptive. The figures you take to be children are sometimes so; sometimes adults; the animal is exaggerated to denote its importance rather than its real size."

"*The* animal?" I queried. "Just one?"

"Oh yes, it is always a wolf. The coat is usually given an ornamental form, it can look feathery sometimes, but the earliest examples are clearer. Also it is our main wild animal, you know."

I thought of Dark Age Scandinavia and its cult of wolf-masks and metaphors of outlaw; both grim images; of something feared or venerated?

She laughed. "There is always the one story. The wolf follows a little girl; he wants to mate with her; but when she refuses, he eats her. Snap-snap! Are you shocked?"

"Why, that is like a French folk-tale," I said. "Let me see ... by Perrault ... about 1700."

"Perhaps. But ask yourself, where were wolves more likely to be found, in civilised France or the wilds around Lupalok?"

I smiled, to show I did not believe that wolves still behaved so in a people's republic today, and indeed she went on to assure me it was purely legend, the natural resentment of a farming world for a predator and outlaw. It flicked through my mind that the wolf might just as easily serve as a symbol of the Turk, but perhaps it would not be tactful to mention that.

"The wall drawings – and carvings – are always narrative then?"

"Not really, it is very static, the image. Always showing one particular aspect of the story, one stage of the action; generally a chase; never the actual conclusion."

"And does the woodcutter never turn up to save the child?" I asked.

"Perhaps. They change the ending as they like. But the fear of the chase is always there."

"The figures were not running in the versions I saw," I pointed out. "What is the point of running away from a wolf?"

She shrugged.

"A monoculture," I mused. "A Wolf Art. So you are all wolf-people?"

She fixed her green eyes on me. "No, no – it is myth – in reality the wolf never wins!"

After a long day, we decided to rest that evening in our chalet outside the city. A simple meal was available in the dining room, with wine from one of those quaint jugs, with something of a jaw about the spout, and something of a tail in the fashioning of the handle. This reminded me of my trip to the museum, and I told Jenny and Joe something of my discoveries: of the wolf harassing the people, but not the details of the story.

"Lupine," said Joe. "That's the adjective from wolf isn't it? A good name for the city!"

We agreed that walking round and round in a circle or clambering up and down stairs was not a proper entertainment for the morrow. We would visit the River Duba instead and take advantage of the fair weather and the beauty of the countryside. We collected a picnic and joined an excursion with several other English families. Their opinion of the city was not long withheld: "Not a proper capital at all"; "so boring, better in our hotel"; "a joke, having holiday flights here!"; "but the weather makes up for it." A unanimous vote against Lupalok, but not the seething revolt that was likely to spoil anyone's brief stay. Though I could imagine some cutting comments turning up on the internet later.

Despite the poor view of Lupalok held by our fellow guests, we three decided to spend the last evening of our midweek break in the city, at a hostelry of Joe's choice.

This was one large ground-floor room, with rough tables and chairs; all the public bars appeared to be much the same; perhaps the beers were a few dozzos cheaper; if Joe found the barmaids particularly admirable, he would do well to keep it to himself. In fact, they were not in evidence; I half-heard Joe ask the landlord where the "bonnie lasses" were, but the only reply was "it's Thursday." Jenny was the only female present, and "I'll have to talk to you then I suppose" was Joe's smirking remark as he sat down. His defence, "Well I fancied chasing someone tonight," went down no better; but it was just Joe's attempt at humour. The real reason, he explained, was that he had heard there would be some music tonight.

Of a truth, I realised I had heard no music since entering Lupalok: no radios, no jukeboxes, not even a picturesque hurdy-gurdy in the old-fashioned streets. What would it be like? We speculated over our drinks; my supposition that it would be a solo male singer, droning through an epic poem on a monotonous single note was closest to the mark: an elaborately costumed man turned up but a glass or so later; drab or grey was his garb, with many fluttering ribbons or paper streamers that rustled when he lifted his arms. He gave us thoughtful greetings as strangers to his art and looked rather alarmed to see Jenny there, as it seemed to me. A flurry of conversation with the landlord followed (in Lupalokian), leading to no conclusion. Except that he composed his stance and began his oration.

If Joe made an error in planning the evening's entertainment, it was that he had made no enquiry beforehand what the singing would be about or what the words meant. The whole thing was incomprehensible to us, and I was slightly wrong in my forecast about a voice on one monotonous note. It rose and fell with a desperate sobbing, that proved horribly tedious after a few dozen verses. Worse, now the performance was underway, and everyone else attending with respect, we had no opportunity to ask what it meant. It was only the fear of appearing deliberately rude that made us sit out a quarter hour or so of this monstrous ethnic harangue. We needed no chance to talk it over to reach tacit agreement that we would leave at the first opportunity.

There was no break. The story (if story it was) carried on and on, the voice gaining in intensity rather than tiring. Our one hope seemed to lie in the song reaching its climax soon – and then stopping. Which in a way is what happened. The swoops and rises of the voice had reached a new crescendo when the audience, as a man, turned their eyes to the open door. We looked round too, and beheld a large grey animal patter into the gap out of the dark street. It was, we realised, with something of a shock, a wolf. Real! Live! Quiet and apparently charmed by the singing, its pink tongue slightly on one side of its mouth, much as your pet dog might grin at you. (After all, I felt like saying, it is Thursday.) It paused on the threshold, taking in the sound, and when I think back on it, I realise the singing was as much like wolf-music as you are ever likely to come across in the world of men.

The wolf then advanced, entering the drinking room, and slowly patrolled round, as though greeting his old friends. A tame wolf is a contradiction in terms, and my supposition is that only the music held him in check. A sort of wolf trance. Eventually he turned to our corner and padded over in a slow, insolent way that conveyed his absolute feral power over us. He stopped a pace or two off, and seemed to eye Jenny with such longing in his liquid eyes that I hardly noticed the singer abruptly cease. In the total quiet that ensued, I think I heard Jenny give a sharp intake of breath. But neither she, or anyone moved; the wolf was still also, his hypnotic gaze on Jenny unbroken.

Perhaps (I thought) he will go away now. But with everyone stock-still around us, it was clearly very much up to the wolf what he wished to do next, and move away he did not. Joe risked gently putting his fingers in Jenny's wine and flicking them at the beast. It did not have an effect, though the stance of the animal perhaps became tenser at this childish interruption. Now I am very fond of my step-daughter, and became quite resolute I would not share her with a lupine. I reached in my pocket, carefully drew out a box of matches, and struck one, leaning forward to hold it virtually under the beast's nose.

With a sudden yelp, he was gone. It was not only the wolf that I shocked. The singer gave a cry and rushed out, as though I might set light to him too; and everyone round the room seemed to shrink at the sight of fire. I might have laughed if the match had not burned down to my fingers at that moment. In fact, I did laugh (as I recall) in an attempt to break the tension, and with affable signs, shepherded my party out into the street, and hopefully to safety.

And that was the conclusion of our strange holiday in Lupalok. I do not recommend it as a destination.

Yet in a way I learned something. That, practically speaking, it is always the aggressor that wins. His initiative is automatically admired by the other side; his actions copied and adopted as the norm. Even if the attacker loses in a physical sense, as may often happen with those rash enough to start a war, their ethic invades the opposing world where their force can not, and indelibly infects it.

There is no other way I can account for the loss of civil liberties that has dogged our society for the past half-century. As to the future, the mandates against smoking, against dogs, against stimulants; the loss of respect for other cultures and other races; the insistence on competition and humiliation; the joy of zero tolerance and the increasing crudity of our justice system indicate to me the battle on the ground is futile. The wolf need not win: we are none the less likely to turn into veritable wolves.

Sir Gerry Robinson
Businessman and TV presenter

I just wish we could embrace Europe with greater enthusiasm. We always feel on the edge of things, waving frantically from the sidelines.

The European Single Market is a brilliant opportunity. Yes, there are problems, but let's try to solve them from inside the tent.

Adrian McNally

Yorkshire born manager, record producer and pianist for Mercury Music Prize nominated Rachel Unthank & The Winterset, now known as The Unthanks, living in Northumberland and married to Rachel Unthank

Big Fish Little Fish

I hadn't thought much about my vague positivism towards Europe until a recent scrape with a scary Irishman illustrated why feeling European is a natural stance for me to embrace.

It had been an intimidating atmosphere all night. We were setting up the PA in the early evening when the tobacco riddled, prune-esque concert secretary gave me a booklet of dos and don'ts the size of a small novel. He made me read the whole thing before I started sound-checking the band. In addition to technical matters, there was useful guidance contained in their drug policy ("All drugs are the work of the devil. These premises, including your dressing room, will NOT play host to hell") and an ominous clause to inform us that if our volume tripped the decibel-meter or they received noise complaints from neighbours, it was at the discretion of the door staff as to how the matter would be resolved. Best of all was the closing line: "This is an Irish club, expect a warm welcome".

During the second half of the show, the band's bass player received a note, placed on his monitor, coolly delivered mid-song by a genial looking middle-aged man, albeit six foot tall and full of muscle.

Assuming it would be some sort of song request, perhaps for someone's birthday, the bass player was quite surprised to read, "play something Irish, or I will shit on your face". This, despite the fact that the band had playing nothing but jig after reel all night. We knew what it meant though. They wanted a Danny Boy or a Wild Rover. Non of that diddly-diddly crap.

My own brush with the same man who delivered the note came as we were packing up. When the band finished, we de-rigged while loud music carried on through the house PA. I was on my hands and knees wrapping a lead around my elbow when I got a tap on my right shoulder. It was he, bending down to ensure his face was in mine.

"Stand up cunt," he said, in that classic, deep, dead-pan Northern Ireland accent that puts the fear of god into we English. My heart sunk and raced all at once, causing my standing up to be staggered and clumsy.

"What's that mate?" I said. Pretending that I hadn't heard him was about the best plan I could think of to avoid imminent confrontation.

"Have you no fucking manners," he asked. I got a light shower of spittle on the 'k' of 'fucking' and a whiff of whisky that could have stunned or perhaps killed a small mammal. I hadn't a clue what act of impoliteness I'd committed, but whatever it was, it seemed pretty big to him.

"Sorry mate, I don't follow," I said.

"Call yourself an Irish band and you're on your hands and knees while this is playing." With this he gesticulated over my shoulder, and I turned round to find that everyone in the room was standing. Standing to attention in fact; standing I realised, in respect to the Irish national anthem. Bugger.

"Fuck, shit, sorry mate, I had no idea." I had insulted his nation, or his politics, or whatever (I wasn't going to enquire) and he appeared ready to avenge me single-handedly on behalf of his cause. Up to this point, I had managed to get through life without experiencing the contact of a single punch, either received or delivered. I was about to break my duck it appeared.

"Sure, you'd stand up for your own bloody English national anthem so you would." Don't take the Irish lingo as a sign of friendliness. He delivered the line with my shirt collar clenched in his fist.

No! I wouldn't stand for my own National Anthem! Well, I probably would actually, especially if my gran was looking on. But I could say to him that I wouldn't. That might work. I took my chance.

"Actually I wouldn't mate no. It's not my anthem anyway. I'm not English. I'm from Yorkshire."

He didn't exactly burst into laughter and usher me towards the bar to buy me a pint for the confusion. Nor did he retort with "Aha, the Yorkshire man is indeed a breed of his own, Dingle-boy. You northern boys aren't really English at all; you're just like us in fact." He didn't even say "fair play to yer, a Yorkshire man's grand with me, so it is," but he did let go of my collar, he did relinquish eyeball contact, grumbled something inaudible in my direction, and he did leave my nil punch record intact.

I had a similar opportunity to define my northern-ness as being different from being English when I came close to fisticuffs with a drunken Scotsman. Just like my Northern Irish friend, I convinced the volatile young Scot that by being from Yorkshire, I was somehow one of his kind, or at least not the English poof he had put me down for. Indeed I do feel like one of his kind, violent tendencies apart, which gives me a different perspective on being European than the stereotypical Anglo attitude to joining our mainland friends.

I'm a Barnsley boy, born and bred in a small and depressed mining village. Growing up somewhere grim gives you somewhere to escape from, I've always thought. Gives you dreams. Somewhere crap from where to view the pot of gold at the end of the rainbow.

Even so, I have a very strong relationship and sense of identity with my South Yorkshire, and indeed my West, where I have lived for the past 7 years. Yet along side this place that I've found for myself, I have come to feel European too. I am a Yorkshire man. I am a European. I can feel British too, but rarely do I feel English.

My lack of affinity with Englishness isn't related to a lack of patriotism, or the embarrassment caused by the Brits-abroad effect, or those who have hijacked the English flag to promote nationalism and xenophobia. My disaffection with being English has more to do with feeling like an outsider in my own country. That is to say, I don't feel represented by my own country. I'm on the edge somewhere.

The media, culture and government that is supposed to be for me comes from a far distant capital. Growing up during the mining strikes, we all felt like we from a different planet from the powers that ruled us, let alone a few hundred miles up the M1. Much of middle England however; English types who the government and media do provide for; don't feel like outsiders in their own country. Here in lies the crux of why my feelings on Europe, as a northern English boy, differ from many of those English folk in middle England. To me, many attitudes towards being European relate to whether you're an outsider, or whether you're not.

Think of it this way. England is already part of a collective known as Great Britain. It is central to Britain in fact, so why would it want to demote itself to a bit part of a larger collective known as Europe. Scotland, Wales and Northern Ireland meanwhile, are bit parts of a collective (Britain) with a dominant force (England) they do not care for, so naturally they would embrace a larger collective (Europe), with more little outsiders and no dominant single force. I believe that is part of why the powers in Scotland, Wales and Northern Ireland are generally more pro-Europe than in England.

So being prepared to feel European in Britain is related to whether you're an outsider, or part of a dominant force. As a working class Yorkshire man, I have always felt like an outsider in my own country; a country ruled by a capital-centric government and media; therefore I too prefer the notion of a wider collective with more equals.

The Irish, Scots and Welsh all have stronger national identities and pride than the English, while people in parts of England such as Yorkshire, Cornwall, Liverpool and Newcastle (let's call them Anglo-outsiders!) have strong regional identities and pride, but little national affinity. Lack of English pride is often attributed to the embarrassment and guilt of being English caused by our demise from world rulers or by those blurring patriotism with nationalism. I believe it is related more to the familiar position of being central to things. There appears to be a contradiction in my argument, but I am not referring to England's central position in relationship to our former world domination, as that is beyond the living memory of most. I am referring to the central and controlling position of England within Britain. The Irish, Scots, Welsh and Anglo-outsiders have grown up watching news and culture beamed from somewhere distant that doesn't represent them by people who aren't like them. One of the key Euro-sceptic arguments in England is the fear and distaste towards being governed from afar (i.e. Brussels) by people who don't understand our needs. The Northern Irish, Scots, Welsh and Anglo-outsiders have felt this for years and years.

Growing up in Northern England, I have felt the same. When people feel unrepresented and controlled from afar, they group together and develop a stronger sense of identity and pride in order to define their place. Outsiders and underdogs have causes to fight and injustice to bemoan. For as long as the government and media of London and England represent Great Britain, England will remain a big fish in a little pond, disliked by its smaller neighbours. It may enjoy it's dominant position at the centre of things, but reluctant to jump from it's little pond into the sea of Europe it will be unable to grow into the fish it could be, given more waters to swim. I think I've taken that analogy far enough now, don't you?

Thatcher used to bang on about protecting our sovereignty and heritage, but we won't start to celebrate or take pride in our own nation and culture while we're too embarrassed that the cooler Irish and Scots don't like us.

On the positive side, the trend of using presenters with regional accents is helping to dissolve the feeling that we are being represented from elsewhere. Finding a way to celebrate regional and national diversity is part of feeling happy about joining a larger party. England has to understand and be happy with its own multi-cultural identity in order to be chilled out enough to give itself to Europe. You have to love yourself in order to let others love you, as they say.

The devolution of Wales and Scotland has to be a positive step too. I never thought I'd find myself thinking that. It's a silly thing, but I like to support the football teams of those "home nations" as much as I do England, and I get upset and incredulous when those nations don't feel the same way back. It is only now I have stumbled through my theory that it follows that relations between the home nations will only get better when we have fewer ties, not more. The sooner control of the home nations leaves England; the sooner the other home nations will stop feeling resentful towards England for being controlled and under-represented. The sooner England stops feeling like a centre of its own the sooner it will start behaving like an equal player in Europe.

And the sooner I will stop getting punch threats from my Celtic neighbours.

Gisela Stuart

Labour MP for Birmingham Edgbaston

As a modern European – German by birth and British by choice – I am a first hand beneficiary of Europe's freedoms. A whole generation of people now travel and work across Europe, largely taking for granted the benefits they are reaping from the 'four freedoms' which formed the basis of the European Community back in 1957 – freedom of movement of goods, freedom of movement of persons, freedom to provide services and freedom of movement of capital.

These opportunities changed my life. When I came to the UK in 1974, I did not need a work permit, had the right of residence and could go on to a British university. Now after 30 years in this country, I have not only succeeded in learning English, which was the original purpose of my visit to Britain, but am now the democratically elected Member of Parliament for Birmingham Edgbaston. In 1939, the constituency was represented by Neville Chamberlain. Now it is represented by a woman born near Munich. To my children the mere notion of Germany and Britain going to war against each other would seem sheer fantasy. No one needs to convince me that European cooperation has been a force for good. That is why I want to make sure that there is a European Union which is effective and democratic – and which is able to evolve so as to achieve the needs and aspirations of its peoples. I do not want us to become complacent as we seek to shape a new Europe. And that is why I believe that we need a better and more informed debate about Europe in Parliament and beyond.

The Convention on the Future of Europe brought together politicians from 28 countries over a period of sixteen months. The result was a Draft Treaty establishing a Constitution for Europe.

I served as one of two House of Commons representatives on the Convention and as a representative of National Parliaments on the Presidium, the small group charged with putting together the draft. (I was the only woman on the Presidium.)

When I was appointed by the House of Commons I entered the Convention with enthusiasm. I did not prejudge the outcome of the Intergovernmental Conference. But I confess, after sixteen months at the heart of the process, I am concerned about many aspects of the draft Constitution. The enlarged European Union must be made to work better, but I am not convinced the proposed Constitution, as it stands, will meet the needs of an expanding Europe.

Not once in the sixteen months I spent on the Convention did representatives question whether deeper integration is what the people of Europe want, whether it serves their best interests or whether it provides the best basis for a sustainable structure for an expanding Union.

The debates focused solely on where we could do more at European Union level. None of the existing policies were questioned.

There seems, however, to be a problem with making this case if you are a British pro-European. Our reputation as Europe's 'awkward squad' gets in the way. Traditional British ambivalence towards Europe, with a history of hesitancy about every step towards closer European integration before generally joining in the end, has left Britain accused of being 'reluctant Europeans'. Jean Monnet, who led the movement to unify Western Europe in the 1950s and 1960s and is often called the father of the European Community, had his own explanation for this, suggesting: "There is one thing you British will never understand: an idea. And there is one thing you are supremely good at grasping: a hard fact. We will have to make Europe without you – but then you will have to come in and join us."

However, the British reputation is a little unfair. After all, Britain is the only country to have had an application to join the European Union turned down twice. The fact that Britain did not join until 1973 was not entirely its own fault. That we strove to join, voted to stay in and have remained engaged members of the Union does at least suggest some doggedness in our attitude.

And regardless of Britain's record of having missed various European buses or trains, as it is often described, nobody can accuse the present [Labour] government of having been a reluctant participant in the Convention on the Future of Europe. To that extent we have become good Europeans rather than reluctant Europeans. But what does that mean? Being a 'good European' does not mean accepting the status quo or even a consolidation or 'tidying up' of the status quo. Neither does it mean that the European constitution is less important than it is. Peter Hain, the British Government's representative on the Convention, said that, "Three quarters of it [the Constitution] is tidying up". But that still left a quarter that he admitted on another occasion was, "Creating a new constitutional order for a new united Europe".

In the past most politicians have focused on the economic rather than the political implications of the European Union. The debate about Europe's future is a battle of ideas and ideologies. The European Union has always been a deeply political project.

Convention president Valery Giscard d'Estaing and others urged governments not to unravel the document. But we must be clear about what is in both the United Kingdom's and the European Union's long-term interests. These are interdependent. The Constitution would bring together all that has been agreed in the past and would introduce significant new changes to the EU. It will be difficult to amend and will be subject to interpretation by the European Court of Justice. And it would be able to create powers for itself. It cannot be viewed piecemeal; its sum is more than its parts. To assess its implications, we have to look at its underlying spirit.

The Constitution defines not just institutional arrangements, but also the balance of power, values and objectives. This Constitution is unusual in that it also initiates processes for future development with the aim of deeper and ever closer integration. Where integration can be deepened no further, this text has rigid rules as for example in the list of exclusive competences of the Commission. Power at the centre cannot be returned to member states. Where the political climate means that certain ideas for further integration are not yet acceptable, the Draft Constitution creates the structure for a process to develop later. This

Constitution is the most important political issue facing Europe today. The Government does not have to accept it. Enlargement will go ahead and the European Union will continue.

Democratic legitimacy is not mysteriously divined by a group of some 200 self-selected people meeting in Brussels. The details are to be thrashed out and negotiated over. But this is not just a matter for governments. It is also a matter for parliaments and people. We need to make sure that the people agree with the direction their political leaders are taking them. One way or another, the contents of any constitution must be given proper democratic scrutiny and debate.

Without this process of democratic scrutiny there will be a strengthening in the tide of Euroscepticism, not just in Britain but in other countries too. The recent vote in Sweden was not just against the euro. It was a vote against a political establishment that was taking people along a route to they knew not where, and did not like.

Chris Spedding
Musician

The Elephant in the Living Room

A glance at the map sums it all up. Britain is not a geographical part of Europe at all.

And if we zoom out and take a more global view we can see how those 15th and 16th century voyages of discovery plonked the British Isles smack dab in the middle of world affairs, enabling Anglo-Saxons to win (and lose) two separate empires: the first based in the New World; and the second with India as its jewel. Together with forays into Africa and the antipodes, this latter empire was the one upon which the sun was supposed never to set; the empire symbolised for schoolboys of my generation by reassuring splotches of pink on the schoolroom globe. So perfectly were these splotches distributed that a ship of the Royal Navy, or the British Mercantile Marine, would never be more than a few day's sail from a bit of pink for refitting and the taking on of supplies, the better to rule the waves. (During Britain's imperial epoch, chauvinistic cartographers used to exaggerate the size of "Great" Britain on their maps and globes. It still takes quite an adjustment for me, brought up as I was with the distorted version, to see how puny we really are on an accurately drawn globe!)

But let's use our zoom button again, and focus for a while on our tiny cluster of islands off the northwest coast of the European continent. What do we see? Well I'll tell you what we see. Just as we have seen that Britain is separate from Europe, we see that Ireland is also a separate entity from England, Scotland and Wales. Not only is Ireland separate geographically but its natural isolation makes it distinct ethnically, in religion and in culture – the notable exception being, of course, in the north, that protestant enclave in a land where England has interfered for centuries with catastrophic effect. And is still interfering.

If past generations of British colonists can, with relative good grace, vacate such failed experiments in empire as far afield as India and Africa, then why not in Northern Ireland? Eire has adopted the Euro, is happy to be an economically thriving, sovereign part of Greater Europe (but most definitely not a subordinate part of Greater Britain) whereas Northern Ireland is still partitioned with no clear, self-determining voice of its own. Lopped off from its natural neighbour in the south and artificially tacked on to a supposedly "United" Kingdom of which it is only a political, not a geographical part, Northern Ireland's problems didn't even exist until they were imported and then stirred up by the high-handed policies of successive Lords Lieutenant and governments imposed from across the Irish Sea in Westminster.

Shouldn't the United Nations be saying something about all this? Where was the UN when the Normans went over, and when Cromwell paid his little visit? If Saddam Hussein's Iraq was able to bring the might of the USA down upon it for invading Kuwait, oughtn't we Brits better watch out?

Kidding aside, something tells me that we haven't quite got over our empire phase yet; haven't quite evolved, politically, to the stage where we can be part of a United States of Europe.

There were empires before ours. I suppose the Roman Empire was a United Europe of sorts, an Empire of which Britain was, as any history text book will remind us, an "outpost". By the time the Roman Empire had morphed into the Holy Roman Empire, this latter conglomerate was just a part of that larger medieval entity known, up to the Reformation, as Christendom, a loose concept rather than a geographic region, until it was given a purpose and a militant identity by the crusades, which were preached against an "infidel" who, initially, posed no greater threat than occupying the Holy City of Jerusalem. This was probably the beginning of a Middle Eastern crisis which seems to have been with us, in one form or another, for almost a thousand years.

Later came the dynastic squabbles of the 100 Year's War and more recently the ideological wars against the "isms": Bonapartism, German militarism, Nazism, Communism and totalitarianism.

What a mess! No wonder we Brits have often preferred to use our island fortress as a stepping stone to new vistas as far away as possible from the cauldron of Europe. It hasn't always been that way, though. We haven't always had our face turned away from our continental neighbours. Maybe it was our insularity that enabled us to provide some much needed and timely help, which we did on several notable occasions when Europe called upon us. To an Englishman, up to and including the 18th century, the word "Empire" wasn't used to denote anything of ours – what we had in the New World were "colonies". But up to the time of the Napoleonic Wars if an Englishman, or a European, used the "E" word in conversation, he usually meant the Holy Roman Empire, that family concern of the Hapsburgs. It was this Empire which was Britain's main partner in the Grand Alliance against Louis XIV, and we produced the man of the hour, in the person of the Duke of Marlborough, to save Europe from the megalomania of the Sun King. We also stepped up to the plate, alone usually, against similar incursions from Bonaparte and Hitler. So we do deserve a little credit.

Well, that's all over now. The world has changed – the worm has turned. But before we present ourselves on the world stage as a fully politically evolved and United Kingdom, shouldn't we try and do something about that rather smelly elephant in our living room? The one we've been ignoring but won't go away, that dismally failed, outmoded experiment in imperial pretension we call Northern Ireland?

Postscript written after the events of 7/7/05

It seems that we can now extend the elephant-in-the-living-room metaphor. There now lives among us a new kind of terrorist, a British-born one who will go to extreme lengths previously untried by the IRA. For our leaders to talk glibly of the "fight against terrorism" is all very well except for the rather unsettling fact that terrorism is one of the few things that it seems impossible to "fight". Our dealings with the IRA should have taught us that by now. Isn't the way to eradicate terrorism to understand and work towards removing the causes, and rehabilitating those who are feeling disaffected and disenfranchised? Current policy seems to be trying to both fight and understand the problem at the same time! You don't have to have a doctorate in social sciences to know that that can't possibly work – that the one approach will cancel out the other. The parallels between our interference in Ireland and our involvement in the ongoing Iraq war are obvious, and so are the tragic results.

Diana Elder
Architect

The Euro-Nerds Have It; niceness prevails

The Euro-nerds have it; we are going to bring nations together and ensure economic stability; we've based it on the cast-iron, OO gauge premise that if we all have the same values, we won't fight amongst ourselves. We are keeping it simple, infantile even; we'll live in peace and harmony and be forever happy and never say a bad word to each other, never inflict injury or suffer an old fashioned, straightforward tyranny ever again. There will be no losers. We are keeping it simple and all will be well in the end. Let's take out the complications, or even be ignorant of them. We must eliminate all risk. Let mediocrity be our maxim; the world will be a better place. Value systems? It's just likes and dislikes isn't it? It's about knowing who you are and what you want – marketing really. Anyway, clap your hands and rejoice; the meek have inherited the earth!

The nerds have it! That's so nice – check out our greetings card manifesto. We will all learn the same stuff by the same method – a smattering of education will be sufficient. Let's all earn a living in the same way in order to live the same life so no-one feels left out. Let's all use the same technology so we can really communicate meaningfully and make progress our watchword – distance ourselves from the past – it was a real mess! We should eat the same food produced in the same way – it's a fundamental human right! If only we could all live in houses which are all the same – cheap to produce and we'll all feel equal – then we can fill them with the same spoils of our shared labour bought in towns which are all the same; hypermarkets and drinking galleries, with the odd remaining Chateau or Schloss or Cathedral to lend a slight sense of history, as long as it avoids of any connection to those gruesome wars that kept accentuating the differences between peoples. Two minutes silence every day for every single person who has ever died; seems the right thing to do – or maybe a scale of grieving – the more recent victims get more minutes? Anyway, let's consign nastiness to the past; be nice to each other – show your emotions! Weep if you want – but don't get angry – that's no use.

Consume now – pay later; a little debt makes the financial world go round! We need to keep consuming; anything and everything – what kind of a world would it be if everyone stopped consuming? Not very nice.

We can all have the same colour of politics too; we favour the one size fits all paradigm for its simplicity; no decisions to be made, no thinking required, no terrible dilemma – choice is all too difficult – eliminate choice to gain freedom – it's really nice – a fluffy kitten of a notion.

We need to have quality time to talk about the same things and preoccupy ourselves with the same simple issues. When all is well with our world, we won't need to think deeply about anything other than lifestyle – how nice is my house, how nice is my garden, how nice do I look? (No deeper examination required for nice people). This is great! This is easy! If everything is uniform, it is all so simple – the freedom of one size fits all. The nerds have it! It's truly nice – an executive home in the suburbs kind of a future.

There is of course, some nice, neat reasoning behind all this; catering for the individual is a drag; it requires some really creative thought – it is difficult – too difficult – not very nice. Individuals cause no end of problems – sniping from the margins, foisting their insane views on us, complicating everything, asking too many questions – just be calm! We understand that human beings are complex little souls – contrary and troublesome – a bit like small children and difficult adolescents – suffer them to come unto us and we will show them the way! Render it all down to nothing; do not hurl ourselves into any several world – therein lies danger.

You have to remember that everything is getting nicer all the time. To the nerd, even the ongoing greatest irony that those who desire to be in charge are the least able to carry out the task, has an inherent niceness to it; those leaders of ours, being nice enough, kindly fit their objectives to their lack of capability and convince themselves, for our benefit, that they have all the skills and judgement and worldly experience to get the job done. Captains of industry with no leadership qualities, just very ordinary people, fall upon nursery strategies; buy cheap, sell at a profit – stack it high – nothing original please – it might make us cry. And if they fail – it's OK because they didn't mean to – all nice people make mistakes – they must be rewarded for failure just as they would be for success; just like anyone else in this scheme, young or old. They are fundamentally nice and deserve to be forgiven.

It's alright if lawyers *manqués* turned politicians run the show. It's OK if they create their own broad and shallow contexts to give credence to their perpetual need to make their mark. As a result, they will hand out judgements designed to test the practical abilities of citizens – it's a non-prescriptive, freedom-laden, self-help kind of world they advocate. Moreover, it confirms they know themselves; that they were once lawyers and have no capacity to adapt – this makes for a more honest relationship all round and we will respect them for it. And if they fail – it's OK because they didn't mean to fail – we all make mistakes – they must be rewarded for failure just as they would be for success; just like anyone else in this scheme. They too are fundamentally nice.

So Nerds are nice and have the best interests of the collective nations at heart – everything they attempt to do is motivated by a desire to be nice and just sort things out without a great fuss.

Let's make the world a nice place. Let's not preoccupy ourselves with things which are not nice. We want to be thought of as nice people – we need to prove that we are nicer than nasty people; everything has to be nice and so anything deemed nasty is not required; nice people don't kick up a fuss, nice people are not disagreeable, nice people don't mind being told what to do. If they do flinch, you just tell them again nicely – and if they still disagree, it's because they are in fact nasty and we must accept that some people are, but nevertheless do everything we can to maintain our ways of niceness and protect ourselves from nastiness.

True nerds can be temporarily nasty out of necessity or by accident – then, they can be forgiven, because nice people forgive fundamentally nice people – it's a circle of niceness.

So the future is nerdish; be glad it is so. Nerds don't start wars – they don't do anything out of the ordinary. It's true we lack imagination and creativity; we are indeed mechanistic, box thinkers, wrapped up in trivia, from dull backgrounds, fearful of the unknown (especially people); we never take risks; we are fundamentally asexual, ordinary, uninterested in truth and beauty, intellectually impoverished. But we are undeniably nice and we are squarely in charge thanks to the technological age and the global village of free trade. This Europe, this hive of commercial activity will be the haven of Accountants, Solicitors, Bankers, Estate Agents, Management Consultants of every hue, Entrepreneurs of all stripes, IT Operatives ... not that each of these professions requires specific and easily definable skills – programmes of de-skilling and skills-mixing, starting at home and honed in school will make all of us all the more equal – the level playing field is our other maxim – what a wonderful world!

So spread the word and shout out the good news from your Euro-rooftops; we are creating a whole continent which is easy to manage and completely process re-engineered; it will be a medium-sized retail outlet with big ideas to suit the simple needs of the citizens. It will have a weather eye on the future and on the world as a whole. Nerds will one day use prototype Europe to rule the entire world and what a nice place it will be – a self-contained warm world where there are no disagreements at all, where never a nasty word is uttered, where everyone could get limitless credit to buy limitless amounts of goods – and we could all speak the same language and have the same values. We will be proud to all look the same as each other; we'll be as obese as the next citizen but comfortable in our common designer draw-stringed leisurewear; proud to be following a media led manual of nerdity accessible to all on the www.

Imagine; all over the world an amalgam of niceness, mediocrity, and uniformity which will guarantee peace in our time. We will all be friends – no, really! How nice.

Neil Bunting
Artist and writer

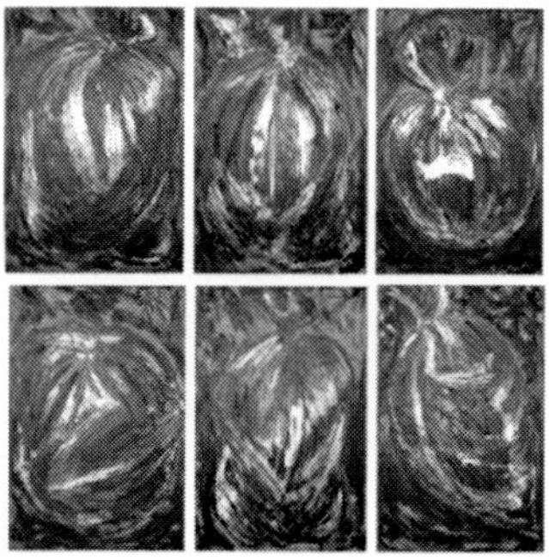

Black rubbish bags – simple, aesthetically lacking, monotonous objects – line the streets of any city, anywhere in Europe; or indeed anywhere in the world. They are commoner currency than the Euro – yet often we fail to notice them on our travels, amongst all the exotic references of language, odour and logo that define a nation's character. We dismiss the bag as a blot on the cityscape, which we would like to digitally erase in Photoshop, along with tourists, rain and fast food chains, as we seek an authentic and quaint world of sun-drenched piazzas, cobbled streets and authentic bars filled with locals.

Wherever we go bags lurk on street corners like pimps; they send a shiver down our spine. They may look lazy but they display surprising plasticity; part of the rapid escalation of the world. We fear being left behind.

We want the world to stand still captured in a freeze-frame, but it won't. We want the Greeks to be olive-skinned and wrinkly from labour, and to hold crinkly drachmas and we want the Italians passionate for pizza with piles of lira in their loving hands.

But things are constantly changing. There is no time for hanging onto things. Bags are being dumped every day. Places are shredding their identity and throwing it away. No one wants to stay where they are. They want to lay down routes not roots.

Chas Hodges
Musician, half of Chas & Dave

We believe that the UK's relationship with Europe is a step forward in bringing the world closer together, and so helping to achieve for our future generations a more peaceful world.

Garry Bushell
Journalist, freethinker

Everything about the European Union is Wrong

At best it's a monstrous folly, at worst a shabby confidence trick hoist upon the peoples of Europe by (let's be generous) misguided politicians.

Ted Heath promised us we were joining a trading block. He knew full well that the real long-term aim of the 'Common Market' was to transform itself into a fully-integrated federal state. The EU was never meant to be a Europe of co-operating brother nations, but Europe A Nation (ironically an old Mosley slogan); and not a free nation either.

Today's EU is an arrogant bloated bureaucracy spewing out endless unnecessary red-tape and regulations. Corruption is rife, wastage obscene.

Naturally I cheered when French and Dutch voters gave the v-sign to the EU constitution in 2005.

But will Europe's integrationist elite take notice? Past experience suggests they will shrug it off and carry on eradicating every aspect of national diversity and sovereignty.

They are our masters and they know what is best for us.

When the French voted 'Non', Peter Mandelson dismissed their verdict and spoke haughtily of a second referendum being organised to deliver the right result for the Brussels mandarins.

Tony Blair's response to the Dutch vote was to immediately postpone Britain's own referendum – even though he had repeatedly promised us one.

Well, we can't vote against it if we never get a chance to vote. Problem solved.

This slippery weasel approach to democracy is to be expected. The EU has been built on dishonesty. The British were lured in under false pretences thirty years ago and we have been misled about every significant change to its workings ever since.

You can understand why the political elite have shamelessly pursued this deceitful agenda. In many ways it was a noble dream. After two fratricidal wars, the idea of building a Europe united by common aims and institutions, a new Europe free of territorial tribalism became a kind of political Holy Grail. And if they have to double-cross a few million simple voters to get there, so be it.

Like the Bolsheviks, they believe the end justifies the means. And like the Bolsheviks, they have failed to deliver anything like the end they promised.

Tragically, at the end of the 20th century when Eastern Europeans were finally celebrating their liberation from oppressive state bureaucracies, Western European politicians were busy constructing their own Stalin-ite equivalent.

The European Project has turned into a classic example of "the evil good men do".

It's remote, and unaccountable; dictatorial, slow and inefficient. It's contemptuous of democracy, debate and tradition.

It's very hard to see what good membership has done for Britain. It's probably best not to ask our farmers, or our fishermen, or our small businessmen when they're busy filling their VAT returns.

I don't take a jingoistic, Sun-style attitude to Europe. I love the place. It's rich in natural beauty and richer still in cultural achievement. But European politics are another matter, and the European Union is a bureaucratic nightmare that has to be killed dead if Britain and England are to live.

Power in the 21st century is increasingly in the hands of multinational corporations and supranational institutions. The only alternative is to rebuild local democracy, cut back the strength and size of the state, slash back taxation, celebrate national diversity and return power to the people.

Attila the Stockbroker

Poet and songwriter

www.attilathestockbroker.com

I have been asked to give my thoughts on the UK's relationship with Europe. I have always been astonished how the question arises. It's like asking me about my relationship with my arm.

There are five continents. Asia, America, Australia, Africa and Europe.

The UK isn't in any of the other four, is it, UK Alchohol Dependence National Socialist Office Workers' Party? Is it, *Daily Mail, Express, Sun* reading amoeba heads? Did you DO geography at school? Inger-land, Blighty, whatever, depending on your social background and chosen form of address (and England is the only bit you actually care about, isn't it?) is in YUR-OP. We – that's all of us – are indisputably, implacably EUROPEAN!

We are. And there is absolutely nothing you can do about it. The only kind of relationship the UK has with Europe is the kind you have with that lager-filled beer gut of yours, or your gout, or the nasty disease you caught from your butler, or if you're a true member of the aristocracy, a member of your close family. We are part of Europe, as they are part of you. You might not like it ... but we are!!

That's right. When your single functioning brain cell is finally switched on, you will eventually realise that this country is as much part of Europe as France, Liechtenstein or any other of those strange places where the inhabitants speak a language which you don't understand! We are European. Like every other country in Europe. One among many. Not special. Got it? The only way we are special is that we're the only country in Europe where 90 percent of the population can't speak a foreign language.

As for the EU: I am for a European Union of the people. I am against a Europe dominated by slimy pinstriped capitalist scum. But then, I'm against a world dominated by slimy capitalist scum, and it most certainly is right now. So, in the same way that the UK isn't a special case in Europe, Europe isn't a special case in the world.

On that basis I LOVE the EU and ADORE the Euro. Why? Because they wind up xenophobic, barathea blazer wearing, chip guzzling, knotted handkerchief brandishing, "Isn't it hot?" complaining, Bernard Manning-loving, PC as a term of abuse-using, football as an excuse for right wing violence-using IDIOTS! Ban the pound! Abolish the English Channel! Superglue the UK to France, right in the middle of the garlic growing region! NOW!!!!!

Mic Dun D
UK Gonzo Rapper/Urban Poet
www.omnimoda.com
www.myspace.com/micdund

Euro Style

Entering Europe but showing my passport
"you won't have to change money mate – you got my support"
stag-nights in Brittany via Isle of Wight link
Portsmouth to Turkey think how cheap the drink
but we're a part of Europe anyway
but not like Spain
we got a blue channel fence
The Queen's idea of defence
but how can I really comment?
it's only money
I just think cash-points giving you euros abroad – that's kind of funny
prices would be the same as say
– Greece – but Greece will have to be as expensive as Britain
no more cheap spirits
no more 18 to 30's getting bitten – gutted

John Edmonds
Senior research fellow, King's College London, formerly general secretary of the GMB Union

Waiting for the New Generation

The European Union is the cause of enormous frustration across the British political spectrum. Eurosceptics talk of conspiracy and long to expose the plot to usurp national sovereignty. Those of us who are regarded as Europhiles believe that the EU is deeply misunderstood, and ache to correct the false impressions put about by the tabloid press. Meanwhile, the British public remain ambivalent: prepared to support the EU in principle while disagreeing with so much of what the EU does in practice.

Amidst such controversy, the enthusiasts on each side seem to agree on one thing: Britain needs a great debate and even a Referendum to settle the issue once and for all. If it cannot be on the Euro, let it be on the Constitution. Wiser heads shake discouragingly. We last had a great debate and a popular Referendum in 1975. That gave us an answer but signally failed to close the issue.

The Eurosceptics complain that Britain's decision of thirty years ago was based on a false prospectus. UKIP and some members of the Conservative Party claim that we were encouraged to join a free-trade area and were deceitfully sucked into political union. This might be a convenient way of re-opening the question of British membership, but there was no deception. Jean Monnet and the founders of the European project trumpeted its political purpose and the Treaty of Rome expressed the aspiration to political union in terms of unmistakeable clarity.

Unfortunately British governments have fed the illusion by being extraordinarily coy about the political purpose of the EU. We know, because politicians have told us so often that the EU will not be allowed to become a European Super State or a United States of Europe. However, I cannot remember when a government minister of either party last explained exactly what level of political integration was favoured and why. UK prime ministers always seem to be ambiguous and defensive. Mrs Thatcher supported the single market and entry into the ERM, but failed to accept that such profound economic changes had to be matched by substantial political development. Mr Blair signed the European Constitution and favours entry into the Euro but failed to make much of a case for either.

What angers the Eurosceptics and infuriates us Europhiles is that British governments consistently fail to take responsibility in Westminster for what they agree in Brussels. For good or ill, EU policy is made in the Council of Ministers where the UK has a veto on some issues and, under qualified majority voting, a weight of vote that gives every British Minister a ready opportunity to block or delay any uncomfortable proposal. Yet the extent of this British power is scarcely mentioned. The scenario most favoured by Number 10 spin-doctors is of wicked Europeans plotting something nasty while gallant little Britain struggles bravely to resist.

With such fairy tales in circulation, it is not surprising that the EU is seen as a malevolent force alien to the British political system. UK politicians frequently tell us that the EU fails to connect with the citizens of Europe. It is hardly surprising. The institutions of the EU are out of date and undemocratic. The Council of Ministers meets in private, the European Parliament has little power and the vacuum has been filled by an un-elected Commission. Instead of making a strong case for modernisation and democratic reform, UK ministers seem comfortable with a system that screens them from responsibility and offers no effective challenge to their authority.

At first sight it should be easy for the governments of the EU to agree that an elected European Parliament should have the normal democratic powers to initiate legislation, to scrutinise the work of the

Commission and to dismiss individual commissioners whose performance is found to be wanting. But this would mean a substantial shift of power from member states to the EU. Thus far every UK government has taken the narrow-minded view that protecting British ministers is more important than enhancing the democracy of the European Union.

It is not just governments that are jealous of their authority. Since 1975 the House of Commons has been determined that the European Parliament should be kept feeble and, whenever possible, cut down to size. Too many backbench MPs at Westminster regard Members of the European Parliament as second-class politicians and want to keep them in that subservient position.

With so many barriers to reform, it is distressingly easy to conclude that the EU will just have to continue simply muddling through. Because of the history of the past thirty years, any UK government would find it difficult to take the lead in rescuing the EU from its torpor. The tragedy is that the fiasco of the European Constitution also makes it doubtful whether any other government in the European Union has the power and moral authority to propose a credible way forward.

The problem is that so many citizens of Western Europe are unhappy with the way the European project has developed. They seem particularly disenchanted with the kind of top down 'take it or leave it' decision-making epitomised by the Giscard D'Estaing Commission. What is needed is a genuinely democratic discussion about the future of the EU, with a level of popular engagement that has been rarely found in the Europe of the last twenty years. This requires the development of new forms of debate with political leaders expanding the terms of discussion rather than attempting to limit its scope.

Are the current European leaders up to the task? It is difficult to be optimistic. So we have to wait for a new generation of political leaders who understand that the EU must be democratic and accountable in a way that, until now, it has never been. The aim should be a Europe of votes rather than fixes where the Parliament becomes more powerful, the Council of Ministers becomes more open and the Commission is subject to greater scrutiny. In the meantime, the best that people with goodwill towards the European project can achieve is to ensure that this difficult transitional period is a time of consolidation rather than disintegration.

Tom Sykes
Writer of fiction and articles for magazines and anthologies in the US, UK, Canada, Australia and Southeast Asia; his 'Ringroad to Immolation' was named one of the best online short stories of 2004 by StorySouth.com; he has co-compiled and edited three travel books, the first, No Such Thing As A Free Ride? *(2005) was serialised in the London Times and named* The Observer's *Travel Book of the Month; and he is a regular columnist for the arts magazine* Quill *which has a circulation of 20,000 across Malaysia and Singapore*

Island Monkeys and a Hidden Unity

As we neared Budapest, I felt like I'd been the subject of an experiment depriving human beings of sunlight, fresh air and basic comfort. Well maybe I exaggerate with retrospect. I'd got my 'coach legs' the previous year on an A-Level tour of Eastern Europe, when marathon crossings of entire countries were punctuated by marathon *wodka* sessions. As some of us hallucinated, some of us copulated and others passed out head-first into toilet bowls, I'm sure something trite like *you can take the kids out of England but you can't take the England out of the kids* crossed the minds of our teachers. On the same trip I was berated by a fellow student for giving the price of a sausage (about 8p in English money) to a child-beggar. "You'll only encourage them to be lazy," she scoffed, as if people dress in rags and contract skin diseases because it's easier than getting a job. It turned out that *her* sole purpose for travelling 650 miles across the continent was to buy a Levi's T-shirt she could easily have bought in Portsmouth City Centre.

Whether it is an English trait to behave abroad exactly as you would at home I don't know. My anecdotes are writ small when compared to Club 18-30, when Spanish communities were annexed by English idiots to lay on English beer, English fish and chips and English music.

I hoped I took a different approach to Ms Levi. I was mightily interested in the history of the region, especially the tumultuous Cold War period, and tried my hardest to see things from the standpoint of Eastern Europeans. I came to respect and admire the people of Prague and Krakow and the former East Berlin; they were people who had emerged optimistic from a long dark night of authoritarianism.

When my three friends and I staggered out of that coach in Budapest we encountered the best and worst of attitudes to foreigners. We were greeted by a spivvy, slick-haired taxi driver wearing Aviators and looking like an extra from *Grand Theft Auto Vice City*, ready to extort shopkeepers and shoot cops. In our lethargy we foolishly got in his car and explained what hotel we needed to get to. When we found ourselves cruising through the countryside it became clear that the driver had absolutely no idea where he was going ... and the meter was racing like a Telethon total. We were finally dropped off in a field and forced to part with a third of our collective budget. This was bad. Half-dead from the coach trip and the Mediterranean heat. Ripped off and stranded Christ knows where.

After some walking we spotted a woman washing a car outside a plush house. We asked her where roughly in Hungary we had ended up and how on earth we might get to our hotel.

She looked troubled and said, in pretty good English, "You see this hill? We are this side of the hill. The hotel is right over *that* side of the hill."

Amazingly, and I will never forget this act of generosity, she not only gave us cold drinks but drove us all the way to the hotel. I tried to imagine an equivalent scenario in Portsmouth, us as Hungarian visitors. We probably would have been told to fuck off.

For a long while I believed the EU to be the solution to xenophobia. Just as the mounting presence of black and brown faces on British streets have made the Alf Garnett position untenable, I thought greater exposure to other Europeans would stop us hating them so much.

But people are losing faith in this artificial Union. Positive social measures such as the minimum wage have been outbalanced by corporate imperatives – 'integration' has simply made it easier for business to exploit and expropriate. After all, the EU evolved from a Franco-German trade agreement over coal and steel in 1950. The autocracy of the Commission and the manner in which failed politicos are booted there (Kinnock, Patten, Mandelson?) should concern anyone who believes in democracy. Eurocrats hypocritically denounce corruption in the Third World while ignoring the corruption on their own doorstep.

A European Union along cultural and social lines, designed for the good of European people rather than small sections of those people, is far more desirable.

As a teenager whenever I met French, Germans or Dutch of my own age there was a supranational understanding between us. We liked the same music, we wore the same clothes, we ate the same food, we had similar progressive outlooks on politics and society. You might call this globalisation but it runs deeper into the fabric of our respective languages and cultures. And deeper still is a common human reason which can allow you to empathise with strangers miles away from your home town or offer lifts to desperate foreigners.

Ben Bradshaw
Labour MP for Exeter

The EU has played a vital role in helping secure an unprecedented period of peace and prosperity in Europe. But it must now undergo a period of radical reform to ensure it has the flexibility and dynamism to meet the global challenges we face.

David Cromwell
Co-editor of Media Lens (www.medialens.org), co-founder of the Crisis Forum (www.crisis-forum.org.uk) and a researcher at the National Oceanography Centre, Southampton, author of 'Private Planet' (2001); co-editor, with Mark Levene, of 'Surviving Climate Change'; and co-author, with David Edwards, of 'Guardians of Power' (2006) and 'Newspeak in the 21st Century' (2009)

Deadly Climate of Consumption

"Is it a present for someone?"
"No. It's for me."

That pang of guilt once again. My personal extravagance this time was a CD by the Dutch guitarist Jan Akkerman, formerly of the famous 1970s band Focus. Shop assistants in the Netherlands often ask if your purchase is a gift. If it is, then it gets wrapped up nicely, perhaps with a little bow. If it isn't, it may still be wrapped up in plain brown paper. The Dutch know the value of good service.

During a trip back to my partner's home town of Groningen, a vibrant university city in the far north of the Netherlands, I was also struck once again by how well-informed the Dutch are about affairs beyond their small, densely-populated land. On this particular visit, I had returned to Holland during Britain's supposed renaissance following New Labour taking power in May 1997. Journalist Bert Wagendorp observed ironically in *de Volkskrant*: "Everything which is modern in the new Britain is given the seal of approval if the word people's can be inserted. [So,] Labour is the People's Party and Blair the

People's PM, Princess Diana is (following her death) the People's Princess, Blair leads the People's Government and the monarchy must, if it wants to survive, become the People's Monarchy. Otherwise Great Britain will become the People's Republic."

And, as Wagendorp pointed out wryly, de Volkskrant translates into English as the People's Newspaper. In a well-written article, he went on to analyse the nation's hopes that had been raised by Tony Blair's stated commitment to serving the people, following eighteen years of destructive Tory rule. This was, alas, before many people came to realise that state support for corporate goals, the repression of civil liberties and the shameful collusion in global imperialism by the planet's most powerful rogue country, would only tighten its malevolent grip under Blair. But, for now, it was a strange experience to see a snapshot of Britain presented so engagingly by a London-based Dutch journalist, while I, a Glaswegian, sat reading his article in a café in Groningen.

When was the last time you saw an in-depth piece about modern Dutch society in a British newspaper? Do not kid yourself that the Netherlands doesn't count. The Dutch are a significant player in a centuries-old business tradition of penetrating international markets and shaping the global economy. Or put another way, Dutch big business is contributing to the fundamental problem of unsustainable economic growth on a finite planet. This drive for short-term profit is being fuelled by global financial speculators, government elites and transnational corporations such as Philips, the electrical goods manufacturers, and Royal Dutch/Shell, the fossil fuel giant (and my former employer; the reason I had lived in the Netherlands for several years).

Such enterprises, backed by a huge public relations industry and compliant media, drive endless consumption. Meanwhile, the planet's natural resources are rapidly diminishing and inequality between rich and poor is spiralling. The primary role of corporate propaganda is to obscure these uncomfortable truths from public view. To take one example, let's switch from Holland to Switzerland for a moment. Consider the astonishing attack on nongovernmental organisations made in January 2005 by Sir Digby Jones, then director general of the Confederation of British Industry. Speaking at the World Economic Forum in Davos, Jones claimed, "The pendulum is swinging too far in favour of the NGOs." He added, "The World Economic Forum is caving in to them. Davos has been hijacked by those who want business to apologise for itself." Much of the mainstream – corporate, in other words – media related this nonsense uncritically.

According to Jones, business is the only route to cleaner water, better healthcare, better education and better roads. "Have I heard that in Davos? Have I hell. We have heard how we are greedy and how we pollute, and how we have got to help Africa. But a celebration of business? No."

Jones was, "fed up with business being characterised as greedy." He went on: "Has anybody ever thought about the greed of the consumer? The consumer consistently wants more for less and business is expected to deliver it."

For the World Economic Forum to be "caving in" under the onslaught of grass roots groups really must feel like the end of the world to those who aim to shape the planet's affairs in their own narrow interests.

But Jones' concern is misplaced. The legal obligation on shareholders to maximise profits in pursuit of endless economic growth, even as the finite planet groans, does face a real obstacle. Namely, that the wealth generated by global capitalism – shared ever more unequally in society – is rapidly being overtaken by the damage that the system itself is wreaking. If existing trends continue, the London-based Global Commons Institute estimates that damages due to climate change will actually exceed global gross domestic product by 2065. We simply will no longer be able to afford living on planet Earth. Global capitalism thus has an inbuilt death wish that will likely take most of us with it; if we let it.

Meanwhile, at the other end of the corporate spectrum, where cuddly business chiefs 'share your pain' at the prospect of climate catastrophe, we find Shell's Lord Ron Oxburgh, shortly to retire at the time of writing. According to Oxburgh, the chairman of Shell's UK arm, governments must take action now to avert 'disaster.' "Whether you like it or not, we live in a capitalist society," he told the Guardian newspaper. "If we at Shell ceased to find and extract and market fossil fuel products while there was demand for them, we would fail as a company. Shell would disappear as any kind of economic force."

Aha! So cracks do occasionally appear in the façade of what passes for reasoned debate in mainstream culture. Awkward insights can sometimes be glimpsed. Yes, we do live in a global capitalist society whose very nature is unsustainable. It demands limitless economic growth; 'growth' which results in terrible damage in terms of human and animal suffering, and environmental devastation.

Oxburgh's argument is that it is up to government "to provide a new regulatory framework that would reduce the incentive to consume fossil fuels." For Oxburgh, and many corporate chiefs, an attractive part of the climate 'solution' is to bury carbon underground. But "the timescale might be impossible, in which case I'm really very worried for the planet because I don't see any other approach."

Oxburgh's comments fit a long-standing pattern of 'greenwashing' propaganda: accept that there is a problem but move the debate away from genuinely sustainable solutions that threaten corporate power and profits. Thus he plumps for the techno-fix, business-oriented option of carbon sequestration "because I don't see any other approach."

Of course he doesn't. Like all industry chiefs, Oxburgh has a blind spot that conveniently overlooks how state-corporate power is relentlessly feeding a suicidal system of globalisation that benefits the few at the expense of the many. Businesses and governments, and their allies in the media and the public relations industry, are fiercely resisting "other approaches" that are being debated and developed by citizens and communities at grass roots levels in Europe and around the world, at such events as the World Social Forum or 'alternative' G8 summits.

It is an uncomfortable thought for the head of a giant oil company, or any powerful enterprise, but whether dangerous climate change can be averted is dependent on the extent to which today's corporate-shaped society can shift to one based on genuine democracy. Tragically, political parties across the world, particularly in the US and UK, are converging like never before under the pressure of big business. As the US philosopher John Dewey once observed cogently, "politics is the shadow cast on society by big business", a reality that has reached epic heights today with the rise of the world's giant multinationals.

Global society is in the grip of a system of economic and political power that views human suffering and impending environmental collapse as incidental to the core issues of revenues generated and costs incurred. But this is not up for discussion in the mainstream media which is an integral component of the capitalist system. It is hardly likely to criticise itself.

Veteran environmentalist Mayer Hillman, author of *How We Can Save the Planet*, notes that the mass media is "complicit in this frightening state of denial." Hillman points out that the "blind ideological commitment to a burgeoning economy is fundamentally frustrating attempts to protect the global environment adequately."

The current targets on reductions of carbon emissions, set by the Kyoto Protocol, are clearly insufficient. Only the policy of contraction and convergence proposed by the London-based Global Commons Institute has a reasonable prospect of success. This is a proposal to ensure a rapid convergence to equal per capita rationing of carbon emissions within an overall contraction of global emissions to an internationally agreed safe level. Hillman likens the present-day emergency to the Second World War when Britain saw stringent rationing of resources.

In order to achieve zero net emissions in the timescale required, governments have to sign up to a global, post-Kyoto framework and take tough decisions on energy use and conservation. But then, as environmental journalist Andrew Rowell observes: "The only moral and rational reaction to global warming is disinvestment in the processing of all fossil fuels."

Governments need to invest massively in energy conservation and renewable energy technologies and building design, by diverting tax breaks and subsidies from, in particular, the fossil fuel and nuclear energy industries. In addition, energy policy should not be in the hands of a few large corporations. There needs to be a rapid shift towards public 'ownership' of energy, just as is the case with water or schools in some countries and in some US states. As solar energy activists Daniel Berman and John O'Connor point out, "Democracy is a false promise if it does not include the power to steer the energy economy."

Whether this genuine democracy springs forth first in Europe, or elsewhere, is not important. But people power needs to become a truly global phenomenon rapidly, before human-induced climate change is unleashed in all its awesome fury.

Sir Teddy Taylor
Conservative MP for forty years

I was a member of Mr Heath's Government as the Scottish Minister of Education when the prime minister decided to apply for membership of the EEC. I resigned my post so that I could vote against the Treaty of Rome and have voted against all the Treaties since then.

My basic concern about Europe is of course that the structure of the EU undermines democracy and I believe very strongly indeed that when democracy disappears the people in a community suffer. There are many other aspects of the EU which concern me including the difficulty in getting unsatisfactory problems resolved like the CAP, but the basic problem is that of the undermining of democracy and we do find now that a huge proportion is dealt with by the European system which means that the views of the community in general have no impact at all.

Simon Woodroffe
Founder of YO!
www.yohow.biz

Europe is One Small Step for the World

One day many years from now our children's, children's, children's, children will look back and wonder at a world in which we had different currencies, when English was just becoming the world's common language and when national rather than common interests bound groups together.

They will still have a loyalty and love of their heritage but it will be just one binding factor of many. Political alliances will no longer be dictated by territorial boundaries.

'Tesco bankrupt after cost of teleportation falls below one rupee' might be a headline of perhaps two or three generations hence. Unbelievable as that may sound to us it is no stranger than the computer, television and electronics age we live in today might sound to our father's father's father's father.

Our first contact with alien intelligence will likely be not space ships landing on earth but a tiny radio signal thousands of years ahead of any physical contact. And what that connection will give mankind is a sense of world community in the vastness of space inhabited by others.

Sixty years after the Wright brothers flew the first aeroplane, man landed on the moon. And that was a period of slow change. What mankind will see change in the next sixty years will surprise even the most vivid imagination today.

The period of civilization since the Industrial Revolution is a tiny microcosm in time, and yet more progress was been made than in any time in history.

And it is in that context that I see the development of Europe. Not to an end in The United States of Europe but a step along the road to The United States of The World.

With that vision in mind, consider a mindset in which we plan not just for the benefit of ourselves in the next ten or twenty years but see our actions and endeavours orientated to the long term future of mankind. Each generation since the Industrial Revolution has been able to glimpse farther ahead into the future than the previous one and today we have an opportunity to be bolder than any previous generation to see a long term world future and to be influenced in some part of our planning by that vision.

To make that more palatable to our own selfish desires for happiness in our own time, consider that the step after the discovery of cures for all disease will, through bio-chemistry, be the prevention of disease through monitoring of health probably as internal implants in the body, from a young age, so that in a few generations life expectancy of 130 years plus with quality of life in old age will be expected. And so perhaps we will live to see the benefits of such long term planning or at least our children and their children will.

The future is invented in the minds of men and women and the experiments, because that is what they are, of living as extended world communities will be the basis on which we will secure world peace, the reduction in the difference between the very rich and the very poor, the elimination of disease and poverty and the security of an eco-sustainable world. In fact a world that most of us in our hearts would like to see but hardly dare to dream.

We can do this by creating extended communities where we work together to understand other races and creeds. It will be messy and may not always serve our short term benefit but the vision that it carries with it and the goodwill and satisfaction it will create in every one of us will be the rewards.

They say human nature is selfish and grasping and that people are inherently unequal, but I believe that the revolution that will follow this current technological revolution will be what I call a Quasi-Spiritual

Revolution. A pursuit of both individual and collective happiness in our times rather than the 'I'm alright Jack', or not as the case maybe, mentality that underlies most of our lives.

Europe is simply an experiment in communal world living that will lay a foundation of understanding for our children's, children's, children's, children who will one day look back and say that was the generation with vision who were willing to go through the beginnings of learning to live as a world community.

One small step at a time and what a legacy to leave behind.

John Redwood
Conservative MP for Wokingham

Too many politicians lied to the British people about Europe. When the UK first joined the Common Market in 1972, people were told we were joining a trading club. Politicians of all parties queued up to assure us there would be no material loss of sovereignty. We had a veto over everything the European Economic Community might want to do. No one could tell us what laws we had to obey or how we were to run our country.

These messages were repeated and reinforced by the Labour government of 1974-9 during the referendum they held on our membership of the EEC in 1975. Most of the campaign was spent assuring us of all the things the EEC would not do or be empowered to do. The government was divided over the issue and used the referendum to garner cross-party support to frustrate its own anti Europeans.

I voted "No" in 1975 because I took the trouble to read the Treaty of Rome, the founding treaty of what is now the European Union. No-one reading that treaty could seriously believe that we were just joining a customs union or trading club. The words of that treaty sketched out the future – ever closer union, political union, monetary union, the indication that the EEC would want to gain more and more power for itself.

The UK joined because of a lie. The British people just wanted to be more prosperous through trade, but the European project was about joint government.

I accepted the verdict of the British people in 1975 and have ever since tried to keep British membership to trading arrangements, which the electorate thought they were approving. It has been a thankless and difficult task, as the push for more and more power has proved strong and the political will in the UK to resist it has proved weak. Those of us who have fought against more and more power gravitating to the continent have had our victories. We have slowed things down and have, from time to time, fought and won important battles. The greatest success so far was to push for a referendum on membership of the Euro, which has prevented the UK from joining monetary union.

Under the Conservative 1979-97 government we had government support for keeping control of our social and employment policy and our immigration and borders policy. These have now been surrendered to Brussels by Labour.

Our campaign to have a fairer deal on how much we pay into the club found a champion in Margaret Thatcher, who obtained a large and continuing rebate for the UK.

Overall, however, we have had to watch and criticise as more and more power passes from democratic national control to bureaucratic continental control. Edward Heath gave away our fishing grounds; Harold Wilson thought that a price worth paying for membership. Margaret Thatcher gave away the veto on certain trade, industry and commercial matters in order to complete the single market. John Major protected the pound through an opt out at Maastricht, but accepted a position on other matters that was to develop into a larger transfer of powers under Labour. Tony Blair, the most pro-European prime minister we had for thirty years, welcomed the EU playing an ever larger role in immigration, crime, anti terrorism, police, foreign policy, defence, energy policy, transport, social and employment policy. More vetoes were surrendered at Nice and Amsterdam than had been surrendered by Conservative prime ministers.

Why does all this matter? Why can't the UK be a 'good partner' and accept the drift of European political life towards a United States of Europe? What is so wrong with the European project?

The idea of European union was born after the disaster of World War Two. France wanted a way of binding Germany in to the peaceful development of the continent. She was seeking reassurance after three invasions in the previous hundred years that Germany would now be a safe and friendly neighbour. Germany wanted to make amends for the horrors of the Nazi period. She saw the opportunity to unite central Europe by peaceful means in a way which did not provoke the neighbours against her. The smaller countries clustered around saw the chance to have a modicum of influence on the policies of the two main powers next door, instead of having no influence. Italy did not want to be left out.

In the late 1940s the idea had merit. Churchill himself was a keen proponent of European union. He saw it as a way of guaranteeing that France and Germany would not go to war again with each other, and as a club for the defeated to rebuild their economies and restore their moral positions. He did not think the UK should join. His vision for the UK was as the fourth force in the world alongside Europe, the USA and the USSR. He wanted the UK to develop her Commonwealth links and ultimately to form a Union of the English speaking peoples with the USA. That is why he wrote a long book entitled *A History of the English Speaking Peoples* rather than a *History of the European Peoples*, and why he concluded that book musing on the form that the eventual union of the English speaking peoples might take.

Today people still argue that the great achievement of the European Union has been to keep the peace in Europe for an unprecedented 60 years so far. This is a grave misreading of the realities of the position. It ignores the dreadful violence and wars in Eastern Europe throughout the last sixty years. Under Soviet domination there were bloody revolts in Hungary, Czechoslovakia and Poland which were put down ruthlessly. After the collapse of the USSR there were a series of damaging wars in the former Yugoslavia. The European Union was powerless to stop the violence under the communists, and intervened in the wars after the end of the communist era, often in an unhelpful way.

Nor can the EU claim the credit for the better relations in Western Europe. Now that Germany is a settled democracy she was never going to invade France, with or without membership of the EU. Furthermore, the frontiers established after the Second World War were in practise guaranteed by the USA, backed up by a formidable arsenal and with US troops stationed on German soil for most of the post war period. If any supranational body should claim credit for the different approach of the new Germany it would be NATO, the defensive alliance which locked the USA into the European political settlement and ensured her forces were available to preserve the status quo. I think more credit should be given to the German people and their governments, who have been peace loving ever since the end of Hitler.

Others argue the case so fashionable in the 1960s and 1970s: that European integration is crucial for successful and fast economic development. When the UK joined the EEC, Germany and France were performing better than Britain. Their growth was faster and their living standards higher. Shortly after we joined, the UK went through a major change of direction of economic policy. Under Margaret Thatcher income tax rates were brought down, nationalised monopolies broken up and privatised, and new laws brought in to regulate trade unions. The UK moved from being the laggard to being the fastest growing of the larger EU economies. We took advantage of flexible exchange rates, our wide-ranging contacts in the five continents of the world and our ability to innovate. The establishment who had argued that we needed to follow the German model were left stranded by the superior performance of the domestic economy.

Their argument was made even more difficult as the German economy got into difficulties in the 1990s following the merger of East and West Germany. The UK has only had one poor period of economic performance between 1981 and 2005 – the two years when our economy was wrecked by membership of the European Exchange Rate mechanism at the beginning of the 1990s. Linking ourselves to the Deutschmark, as the defeatist establishment in the UK was keen to do, gave us first high inflation and then a bad recession. It was bound to do so. There was no right rate for the pound against the Deutschmark. The UK needed its own financial and inflationary discipline. It could not obtain it by coat-tailing on the Germans.

Today, few argue that joining in the full scheme of political union can transform our economy for the better. The business lobbies who were so keen on more European involvement in the 1980s and 1990s have learned a salutary lesson from the disaster of the ERM policy. They also now realise that the EU is a legislation machine, putting more and more rules in the way of their activities. Instead of helping companies become more competitive, the EU imposes costs they do not have to pay in India, China or the USA, making the EU a less and less desirable place to do business in. The UK government's inability to make the case to join the Euro is eloquent testimony to the changed mood. The Euro is the EU's ultimate scheme for full scale union in the economic sphere. The main countries locked into it have struggled to grow. Most people in the UK realise that losing the power to settle our own exchange rate and interest rates would damage us as surely as the Exchange Rate Mechanism damaged us.

Now the argument about the wonders of European Union gravitates more to the advantages of the EU becoming a major force in world affairs. We are told that the UK would have more clout in the world if we subsumed our foreign policy and defence into a European Union. We should be aware of the dangers of this strategy.

It will put us into argument with the USA. The EU has already annoyed the USA by its different approach to the Middle East. France helped Russia arm Saddam Hussein, and did her best to stop the USA removing the dictator. More recently France has sold a 20 percent stake in the Galileo spy in the sky project the EU has established, to China. Most commentators believe Galileo is meant to be a rival to the US system of military surveillance, as well as having civilian uses. The USA does not want China gaining access to the latest military technology and intelligence. France and Germany have widened the rift by agreeing on the need to lift the arms embargo the whole West imposed on China following the events in Tiananmen Square.

Some will say it is a good thing that the EU sometimes stands up to the USA. They think the world needs a counterweight to the USA, a power which could prevent the USA embarking on dangerous military adventures. Unfortunately, the EU will be strong enough to annoy the USA, but not strong enough to stop her. No-one believes the EU's opposition to the war against Iraq made any difference to US strategy. Had the UK been unable to help owing to EU control over our policy, the war would still have gone ahead with the same inevitable conclusion, given the power of US weaponry. The EU knows it is far behind the USA in its military capacity. That is why it has established an Armaments Agency to supervise the rearming of the Union, and why it is developing the Galileo project and new weapons programmes. However, the EU will not spend sufficiently to catch up with the USA.

The EU has many more men and women in arms than the USA, but it lacks the ships, planes, surveillance systems and smart weapons to deliver its force anywhere in the world in the way that the highly mobile and powerful US forces can manage.

Nor can I be impressed by the claims that the EU is needed to tackle crime and terrorism. The EU has used the dreadful terrorist events in the USA, Spain and Indonesia to claim that we need a common system of police and justice to track down the perpetrators and deter the would-be terrorists. Just as the EU held out the prospect of eternal growth and economic success to wrestle powers over the economy from us, so it will use the spectre of terrorism worldwide to demand more and more powers over our criminal justice system. There is no evidence to support the idea that a united Europe will be a Europe better protected against terrorism. Indeed, unfortunately, a strongly centralised Europe is more likely to harbour home grown terrorists, as extremist groups who do not like Brussels rule turn their murderous attention to the Union itself. We have seen the dangers of Irish, Basque and Catalan terrorism in the EU in the last twenty years, directed at national governments the groups do not like. How will the new Union prevent that, and avoid becoming the object of evil groups using murder as a weapon for political ends?

The British people will soon have a chance to decide whether they wish to plunge headlong into the final acts of political union or whether they want a different future for our country. To me the decision is an easy one. We want to trade with our partners in the EU, and be friends with them, but we do not wish to be governed by them. As the others seem determined to complete a Union, with highly centralised government in Brussels having an influence over everything and controlling most things, we have to say "No".

We should offer to let them go ahead with their union – for they need our permission – if we may restore our right to govern ourselves in the important areas of foreign and defence policy, immigration and asylum policy, fishing, agriculture, overseas aid, regulation and monetary affairs. The Labour establishment will tell us such a deal is not on offer. We should reply that of course it is – the EU needs us more than we need them, and they need our permission to go ahead with their mighty project. It is time for the UK to admit the truth. The British people have no intention of burying their governing system in a greater

Union. We will be friends with them and trade with them. It makes sense for both sides to see this, and to sort out the basis on which it can best be done. That will have to happen.

Joe Gordon

Bookseller and blogger

Europe – what do I think of it? What do I think of other Europeans? We're all having to consider these matters, from the wind-blown Shetland Islands through the Baltic down to the warm climes of the Mediterranean. It is a particularly interesting question for a Scot; after all the Scots have been involved, for good or ill, in a geopolitical union for nearly three hundred years (four hundred if you count from the accession of James VI to a new British throne and the Union of the Crowns).

Discussion of Scotland's role within the Union and her relationship with the other kingdoms covers three hundred years of often heated debate – and we're still debating it! Anger over a loss of our parliament to a larger British institution was tempered with the realisation of the increased opportunities available to those living in a now united island nation. History has shown just how many Scots took advantage of those opportunities; soldiers, explorers, missionaries and settlers spread throughout the whole of the British Empire (one reason why there are five times as many people of Scottish descent around the world than there are people living in Scotland).

Naturally there were downsides to this union. Many Scots felt that their role as an equal partner in the Union was not taken seriously – the Scots voice was not heard properly; we were not represented properly in Parliament. With so many artists, merchants and politicians moving to the new centre of power in London, our cultural life was in danger. Gaelic culture went into a decline and Broad Scots seemed to be fading too. The role of Scotland and its place in the Union and the world was questioned by many, from everyday citizens to Sir Walter Scott. Scots worried that their people would become simply homogenous with the other people of the United Kingdom.

And yet Scotland did not lose her unique cultural heritage within the Union. Robert Burns and the man who so inspired him, 'heaven-taught Fergusson' wrote in our Scots tongue and was loved for it (and still are, all around the world). Scott delved into our deep history to great acclaim. And at the same time we created new culture in the shape of the Enlightenment: arts, humanist philosophy, politics, economics, science and engineering – the Scottish contribution in these fields is considerably out of proportion to the size of her population and distant geographical location. Old and new melded together and spread out to others in different lands. Educated gentlemen in Paris salons discussed the work of David Hume while Edinburgh citizens discussed Voltaire as they sipped their fine, imported French claret.

In the last few decades we have all had a new form of identity to consider, that of Europeans. But is this really the new identity that many think it is? Look at the examples I mentioned earlier. The free spread and interchange of ideas during the Enlightenment illustrates how much different Europeans have in common. The ideas of the day were translated and re-printed into French and German and Dutch and so many other languages; discussed, debated, altered, countered, proved, disproved, feeding back into each other and powering a spectacular flowering of intellectual exploration as they criss-crossed the map of Europe.

This was in no small amount thanks to the genius of Mr Gutenberg's invention – another idea which had spread across the cities of Europe centuries earlier. And before Gutenberg there were the monasteries – the information superhighway of their day, crossing all of Europe from remote Scottish isles to the hills of Tuscany. Then there were the merchants – those claret drinkers in Edinburgh had been importing and exporting goods to Europe for centuries. When Wallace fought for Scottish freedom, letters were sent to European partners to tell their merchants that, once more, ports such as Leith were open to trade with the Low Countries and German markets. Norse longships with their fabled navigators sailed from the fjords of Norway right down the

Danube, or around France and Spain to pass through the Pillars of Hercules to the blue waters of the Mediterranean.

We can go further back than this of course. The Celts, the people from whom Scots descend, had a pan-European culture long before the rise of Rome. Not, of course, in the form of a united state or empire, but in a Europe-wide society of peoples connected by many shared cultural traits and beliefs and yet also with many differences to one another; similar but different and all equal. Our history together is far deeper than the modern concept of nation states; we share so much in common, not least our basic humanity. As president Kennedy once put it in more modern times, "We all breathe the same air".

Yet we also have a number of differences. The French view events differently from the English, who see things differently from the Scots or the Germans or the Spanish. Sometimes it seems a miracle we can agree on anything! I believe we should not hide these differences anymore than we should hide our shared qualities – properly channelled and discussed our differences can be an engine for debate and change. Besides, who wants to live in a society where we all think and act the same? And are our national differences really so different from the differences between individuals? In any beer house in Berlin or pub in Glasgow I'm sure you will find as diverse a range of opinions on a variety of subjects as there may be between nations. The fact that we discuss these differences is in itself a sign of our greater shared nature; differences discussed can make us stronger, more perceptive and ultimately closer. As another great figure of the 20th century, Mr Spock, once put it, infinite diversity comes from infinite combinations; our differences are as important as our shared culture.

My personal attitude to Europe is also marked by a mixture of shared values peppered liberally with difference. I recall my former psychology lecturer once telling my class that one of the keys to understanding human behaviour was to comprehend that we were all driven by two different – almost opposite – desires: the need to belong and the need to be apart. We want to be a part of a group, a family, a community, a nation. Yet we also feel the need to differentiate ourselves as individuals – to stand out from the common herd. Nations are composed of individuals, so it should not surprise us that the French may wish to participate in Europe but also worried about a perceived erosion of their own cultural identity. It is not so very different from the concerns of Scots of the eighteenth and nineteenth centuries – the desire to be a part but also to be unique.

The more I consider it the more I realise that I have two different concepts in my mind when I think of Europe. There is Europe the geopolitical entity, a generally benign but sometime bumbling institution which I and a lot of people around Europe like to poke fun at. I despair when they spend vast amounts of time and money on deciding the exact proportion of cocoa a chocolate bar must contain but applaud them when they create something like the European Convention on Human Rights. In that respect I view the European government in similar terms to the way I perceive the Holyrood or Westminster governments – the fact it is based in continental Europe really doesn't make much difference to me, it is the actions it carries out which concern me.

However I've come to realise the Europe I really think of, the Europe I really know is based on the individual level. Living in a vibrant European capital like Edinburgh I have studied, worked, eaten and drunk with friends from Norway to Spain and enjoyed every minute; sharing with them has enriched my life. In the virtual world of email, websites and blogs again I have made contacts across Europe and the rest of the world. You begin to see the world less as nations and more as composed of people you know (and a lot more people like them that you don't). It's not that cultural identity becomes un-important – I am proud of my Scottish and British heritage – but rather that I've come to realise that national identity and culture are secondary to the common heritage which I share with others; ideas and people meeting over borders physical and virtual. I'm myself; an individual, apart; I am part of a diverse group of friends that spans many lands. I'm content with that.

Ernest Wistrich

Former vice-president of the European Movement

Having served in the Royal Air Force during the Second World War, I witnessed the massive destruction, death and misery caused to millions of Europeans of all nationalities. The creation of the European Union, starting with the European Coal and Steel Community in 1950, has progressively, through integration and growing interdependence, made any future conflict between its members impossible.

Simultaneously the removal of barriers to trade and growing economic interdependence has helped to build prosperity of its people to levels unknown in history. The European Union with a combined gross domestic product well in excess of any other in the world, is now an economic superpower able to play a leading role in combating global poverty and helping the rest of the developing world grow towards our level of prosperity.

Finally the Charter of Fundamental Rights, expresses the values, principles and essential political and social rights of the peoples of the European Union. They are a shining example of a multicultural society, based on democracy and the rule of law, that could provide a pattern for the rest of the world.

The United Kingdom's membership of the European Union has made a fundamental contribution to our own prosperity and, by working with our European partners, strengthened our influence in world affairs.

Judge Jules

Radio 1 and globetrotting club DJ

Quite simply, the debate about Europe shouldn't exist. Or at least the notion that British people don't feel 'European'. Even when we thought the world was dish-shaped and explorers dared not fall off the edge, they were aware we lived next door to France, Belgium, Holland and Ireland. We knew that much, because we'd fought battles against most of them. To question our relationship with Europe is akin to saying that Maryland isn't part of the USA.

The issue of monetary union is divisive. We're right to question the impact on our economy of the removal of control over money supply and interest rates. However, this has been used by the media to fool the chattering classes into a broader 'Euroscepticism'.

Throughout history, mankind has needed other tribal groups at whom to sling its arrows. Different religions and other interest groups fight each other, and this has long served as a convenient diversion from the lack of opportunity and relative poverty that the majority of the population experience in their lives.

This will never change. Those who lack opportunity will always need another group that they consider lower down the social, cultural or intellectual scale. However, other European nations shouldn't be the target, and for most young people, I don't believe they are.

My extensive work travels have taught me that there's a distinct 'Northern European' persona, regardless of national boundaries. Lack of decent weather and outdoor culture has created a region where people drink to excess, chide one another and party like it's 1999. By contrast,

Southern Europeans are more relaxed, drink less and seem to require less release from sunlight deficiency.

Peoples' greatest fear is the unknown. Before the era of *en masse* foreign holiday travel, 'Johnny Foreigner' was a mysterious garlic eating, sauerkraut loving, red wine drinking alien from over the English Channel. The free movement of labour within the EU and the democratisation of air travel brought about by budget airlines, have taught young people how similar we actually are to our European neighbours. Even our perennial foe the Germans are remarkably close to the British persona.

When I read the reactionary rubbish peddled by the *Daily Mail*, the greatest consolation is that its readers are a dying breed, literally. As a younger generation, we're part of a Europe that revels in free movement, travel and exploring the relatively small differences between us and our European counterparts. At a basic level, in the same way that black footballers arguably did more to enhance race relations than a legacy of government legislation, the effect of European footballing imports has been similar.

The mystique of our European counterparts has gone, and with that has withered away the prejudice and feelings of island isolation. I don't believe it's a coincidence that Ireland and Britain's EU membership led to the conclusion of the Northern Irish troubles. Ultimately we'll all see the bigger European picture. There will always be minor regional differences, but within the context of a broader European perspective. It's the future.

Harry Landis

Actor and director

Relationship with Europe

In common with most people, including politicians, I haven't read any of the tracts and agreements which those in the UK pontificate about. However as a great fan of Tony Benn I tended to lean towards the point of view which made much of British sovereignty being lost and rule by Brussels taking its place.

In the last few years though I have to a large extent come round to feeling that a lot of good can come out of close relationship with Europe.

Perhaps the biggest influence has been my work as president of the actors' union Equity.

The International Federation of Actors has a European wing which meets regularly. Performers everywhere have common problems and the discussions that take place regarding intellectual rights, repeat fees, ethnic and gender equality etc, from which we learn a lot, create a common bond and negate all parochial feelings. We benefit from each other's experiences and our own situation is thereby enriched.

I have been very impressed by some decisions of the European Court of Human Rights that have forced the British government to climb down from some of its actions and to change the law in areas that have been seen to be unjust and illiberal. The latest, at the time of writing, is the decision re legal aid for the two people who took on McDonalds. The libel case was considered unfair and the law of libel will be looked at again. Some people complain that it is socialism by the back door. If that is true, it is OK by me!

PG Lewis
Professor of European Politics, Open University

I spend quite a lot of time thinking about Europe as well as travelling to and from it. Having taken a first degree in Russian Studies, moved to research on Poland and neighbouring areas, and devoting much time to university-based teaching and researching on the politics of central and eastern Europe, I've had strong contacts with that side of Europe for many years. My wife is French, so we spend a fair amount of time with friends and family just across the Channel too. My origins, on the other hand, are wholly British and there was nothing in my upbringing to produce any kind of particularly 'European' outlook. European interests developed within the framework of the traditional English grammar school where, having got on reasonably well with one subject, young people went on to study more of the same. So I progressed from French to German and then Russian – and then to a university course which entrenched my interest in the eastern part of the continent. For all that time I was wholly English – although it never struck me that I wasn't European as well. This is clearly a minority view within the British population as a whole – even though it is now more than thirty years since the United Kingdom joined the European Community (as it then was). Just why my views and feelings about Europe developed in this way I am not at all sure.

But it certainly isn't a very common feeling amongst the British – and perhaps especially the English – as a whole. Just why so few of its inhabitants are likely to consider Britain as being part of Europe is not clear. Citizens of the UK consistently score the lowest of all European countries in rejecting a European identity (according to a Eurobarometer Report in late 2004), being less than appreciative of the achievements of the European Union and its predecessors (only 38 percent thought that EU membership was 'a good thing'), just about the lowest (though ahead of Sweden) in thinking that their country benefits from being a member, having the lowest level of trust in EU institutions (39 percent in 2004) and generally not aspiring to much of a closer union of the European countries. On the other hand many Brits frequently cross the Channel for work and holidays, some half a million own holiday homes in both France and Spain, and most eat 'European' food and dishes that were not available to previous generations. The EU-generated liberation of the economic area that has driven the enormous success of companies like Easyjet and Ryanair has certainly been eagerly taken advantage of and appreciated by many Britons.

For much of the UK population, nevertheless, Europe is still abroad and something distinct from being British – Europe is across the water and 'over there' rather than being something that Britain is part of. The reasons for this are not obvious, although the British are certainly more keen to occupy a semi-detached status than most other Europeans. British history has, of course, long been based on the idea of the island race and for centuries its main policy was to avoid continental entanglements and ensure that no single nation gained supremacy over continental Europe as a whole. There are certainly traces of these sentiments in contemporary national views of the EU, although the historic and geo-political underpinnings of Britain's splendid isolation are now long gone and disappeared far more rapidly than either Winston Churchill or Jean Monnet envisaged in the immediate post-war period. I have dim memories of one Empire Day at primary school – but I think it was a unique event and soon superseded by more modest commemorations of the Commonwealth. After that came the debacle of the Suez invasion, which was clear proof for all that Britain's imperial past was well and truly over.

Britain was no longer a global power as Conservative prime minister Harold Macmillan soon recognised, as he began the first of several belated attempts to join the developing European Community. Popular enthusiasm for the 'European project' was never strong in Britain – though neither was it particularly intense in any other country either.

There is no doubt that European union in the broad sense was always the outcome of the commitment of a select group of visionaries who developed it as a decidedly elite project. In this it is hardly an exception among major international initiatives. Yet of all EU members the British have continued to remain just about the least enthusiastic about Europe and – at least in the views promoted by papers like *The Sun* and *Daily Mail*, whose representative qualities may certainly be seriously doubted – are often profoundly contemptuous and antagonistic to European neighbours. There are some obvious reasons why I do not share these views but there are no strong factors in my background why I should be particularly pro-European. My early years and family background were certainly not particularly conducive to 'European' sympathies.

The part of London I grew up in during the 1950s was very English. There weren't yet many brown faces around, and the main representatives from across the Channel were a few Poles, Hungarians and other central Europeans who had fled before the war. It was all pretty white, although it did not at the time seem as hideous as Greg Dyke was later to think in a related context. It was, on the other hand, pretty bland and often quite boring. It was an attractive idea to go a bit further than Eastbourne or the Essex coast where holidays were often spent. My first journey across the water was with a school trip to Brittany of which memories are not wholly positive, as I recall a fair number of hours spent on a windy beach with a chill and upset stomach. More impressive was the discovery of the Mediterranean after I had left school. Reaching Genoa and feeling the sunshine of the Italian coast on the night train from Paris was a definite improvement, even if accompanied by the appalling smell of gin left behind by a sailor who had tried (and failed) to drink a whole bottle on the journey and had left a fair bit to slosh around on the carriage floor. The rest of Italy proved to be more fragrant, as did many other parts of the Mediterranean which it was easy and cheap to explore as a hitchhiker in the sixties. Like many others, I felt quite at home there and relished the different ways of life.

Around this time I began to discover Russia and eastern Europe. It was, of course, part of the same continent but it was at the time a very different kind of Europe. The sight in Moscow of many people with obvious family ties with the diverse nations of Central Asia showed how close we were to the edge of Europe and the way of life in Soviet Russia was very different from that depicted in the stories and plays of Chekhov and other classic writers from the 19th century, who certainly depicted a country very different from that found in the 1960s but one that was not so distant from 19th century western Europe. Life in post-Stalinist Russia was another thing. There were certainly some feelings of insecurity and the accoutrements of police state, but any actual harassment only came from black-market money changers and potential purchasers of jeans and sunglasses. Cafes and anything like a pub was virtually unknown, and restaurants generally didn't have much to offer either. But people were friendly and eager to hear as much about western Europe as possible, particularly as they had very little chance of ever getting there.

Life in Poland where, still in the 60s, I spent two years as a graduate student was very different. Cafes there certainly were, as well as some decent restaurants and many colleagues and friends who had few doubts about their European identity but much resentment about the Soviets who had constructed, and were committed to maintaining, the Iron Curtain. It was certainly Europe, but not as many westerners experienced or understood it. And so it continued in much of eastern Europe for the decades that followed – the Soviet-sponsored invasion of Czechoslovakia turned that country emphatically to the west (which had certainly not been the case since the Munich sell-out in 1938) and the rise of Solidarity in Poland that followed 12 years later reaffirmed the nation's faith in its capacity for self-regeneration but also attracted considerable west European support and created strong links that bore more substantial fruit in 1989 and the years of political freedom that followed.

From my point of view, then, the accession of the former communist countries and the emergence of a European Union of 27 members that includes most countries in which I have spent a substantial part of my life is a natural and wholly welcome development. In my view we belong together and form a natural community in major political and moral senses. But feelings and attitudes towards 'Europe' in general are, of course, not the same thing as views that people have about the European Union as an organisation. It is, in one sense, possible to have certain views about Europe in general and quite other ones about the institutions and processes that make up the European

Union and all that goes under the general heading of 'Brussels'. In practice, though, attitudes to Europe and the EU can hardly be distinguished. I could argue that this stems from the general British lack of interest in Europe and ignorance of things European (Eurobarometer surveys consistently show that UK citizens are both aware of their lack of knowledge about Europe and have little interest in remedying their ignorance in this respect). But the situation is not so different in the other countries of Europe, either. Support or rejection of 'Europe' is very much a symbolic process, as the experience of the few countries whose electorate was invited – or permitted – to express an opinion on the ill-fated proposal for a constitution quickly showed.

We are then largely stuck with the Europe we have got – and potentially with the Europe we still want to create. The latter task clearly raises some major uncertainties and practical problems at the present time. It is not at all clear that any more coherent European identity or, to quote a major founding document, an 'ever closer union' is likely to emerge in the foreseeable future. The Germans, French, Italians, Poles and British (whoever they might be) are clearly likely to remain their own people in the years to come, and few people are likely to reject that as a prospect. The main challenge is how to live together – and the general easing of restrictions on travel and mobility conditions in the European area due to the development of a single market has certainly played a part in this. It is not that long ago that the ordinary traveller was restricted to a few French francs or German marks for his annual trip, and that European air fares were among the highest in the world.

To my mind, life is certainly better, richer and more fun in a freer and more integrated Europe – and I am sure that a considerable majority of contemporary Europeans, and particularly the younger generation, feel the same way. But there are certainly a few problems on the agenda – not least how to cope with an EU of 27 members in an association that has blithely ignored the opinions of electors and citizens in many of its major initiatives. It would be a great help if the outdated chauvinist views of some of our popular press were less prominent in this – although most people are sensible enough not to take too much notice of that. On the local and inter-personal level European relations are generally much closer and friendly overall. The lengthy period of peace, increased wealth and mobility throughout much of Europe – far more pronounced, of course, in recent years – have all helped create a shared identity on an *informal* basis, which is for that reason more genuine and spontaneous overall. This is something I welcome wholeheartedly and hope to see develop yet more strongly in future years.

Richard Barrett

Composer

As a socialist I look forward to the time when all national boundaries can be dismantled, together with the corporate monstrosities which exploit them and the state machinery which maintains them.

As an artist, one of my main reasons for leaving England for the continent in 1993 was the insularity and conservatism of British culture, which if anything has intensified in the meantime.

The European Union is of course an alliance of ruling-class interests which (like most aspects of capitalist society) is by no means set up for the benefit of the majority of the population. Therefore its aims and means should be treated with the greatest suspicion. This is not however in any way to excuse bigotry or xenophobia. Cultural differences are fascinating. 'National differences' are poisonous delusions.

I don't feel particularly 'at home' living in Germany where I've lived since 2001, nor did I while I lived in the Netherlands for the previous eight years, but I feel considerably less so in Britain when I go there, despite the fact that my visits are fairly frequent. In other words my sense of belonging to a particular place has been lost. I regard this as an advantage.

Syd Rapson

Former MP for Portsmouth North

My first knowledge of Europe was when my school, Paulsgrove Secondary Modern, arranged an exchange visit to our twin city of Duisburg, Germany. My family had little money but they scraped together the £12/10 shillings fare. We travelled by bus, rail and boat, arriving 18 hours later in Germany, bemused. The food was diabolical – black bread, no tea. It was 1955 and the country was still rebuilding after the war. We were all rock and roll fans but the music was banned throughout Germany. One of my colleagues played the piano in the main school hall thumping out a rock and roll tune which created a riot. We were all in real trouble and couldn't understand why.

I formed a real bond with Duisburg and managed to return 30 years later as a city councillor on the Duisburg Twinning Committee. I viewed Germans as ordinary people who spoke a different language but had a similar outlook. My travels throughout Europe have strengthened my resolve to unite more closely with it. All the young people are the same, wear the same clothes, listen to the same music, have the same optimistic outlook – often the European mainlanders experience higher standards of living than our own. I long for the day when we can ignore the old prejudices and travel unhindered throughout Europe with a similar currency.

I have no fear of my friends in the rest of Europe and believe we are safer in this pact than we would be out of it.

Paul Weisz
Artist

Sir Stephen Wall
British Ambassador to the EU 1995-2000

My Position on Europe

I was always a pro-European for reasons of peace, stability and prosperity which still hold good today. But I did not think a lot about Europe until the referendum of May 1975 on whether Britain should stay in the European Community that we had joined two years earlier.

I was working as a press officer in the Foreign Office News Department. On 14 May, at the height of the campaign, a pretty girl joined our department as a new secretary. She wore flip-flops and a tee shirt with the slogan 'Keep Britain in Europe' across the front.

I have never stopped to ask myself how much of my European conviction I owe to my attraction to that pretty girl. Since she and I have been married for the past thirty years, what would be the point?

Mick Duncan
Secretary of the Anti Sweatshops Campaign – No Sweat

Another Europe

Since the Second World War the main thrust of European governance has been for ever greater convergence. European bosses and heads of state meet regularly to discuss the shape of Europe, to formulate organisations such as the EU and to draw up charters, policies, business agreements, treaties and even a constitution. Often with Britain as the model, they have created a Europe in their own image.

Post-war, the consensus was that some social reform was needed to create stability and growth and to incorporate a disenchanted working class that had threatened rulers with revolution. As the 1945-51 UK Labour Government created the NHS and rebuilt the country, a welfare-statist, Keynesian Europe was built alongside it, at varying paces and through various means, across most of Western Europe. The dictatorships of Spain and Portugal were the – strangely accepted – exception. In Eastern Europe of course 'state-socialism' gave us another model of dictatorship to contend with.

From the 1970s all that started to change. Franco and Salazar are now gone, as is the old Soviet Union. Spain, Portugal and much of the old Eastern Bloc is now part of a New Model Europe. From the viewpoint of a UK-based activist this Europe looks horribly like the New Model Britain – created by Margaret Thatcher, and continued by her ideological heir, Tony Blair – that I have spent most of my youth and adulthood opposing. New Model Europe looks horribly Thatcherite –

low taxation, free-market, anti-union, hostile to outsiders, warlike and increasingly culturally conservative, bland and uninspiring.

It is an irony that the, at best Eurosceptic and at times overtly Euro-hostile Margaret Thatcher should be such an important figure in today's Europe. Yet she is *the* pre-eminent European political figure. Throughout my lifetime, Britain has seen itself as 'in but not of' Europe. It is a daft notion and it is increasingly difficult to understand its purchase with the British Right, when it is 'British', Thatcherite policies that are so dominant in this continent. Yet *The Sun* and the *Mail* still make up stupid scare stories about 'Brussels bureaucrats' and still cast vile insults at mainland Europe – especially Germany and France, and especially when we play them at football. But this mainland Europe is increasingly like the post-Thatcher UK – a racist, petty-minded, free-market, warlike Europe, that is hooked on daft pop songs in limited vocabulary English, US imported movies, dumb celebrities and football. Quite why Britons, and especially the ones who edit our tabloid press, continue to be so hostile to a Europe that is embracing everything they herald in their pages is a mystery. Of course Freud might suggest that this loathing is really a projected loathing of ourselves. But he was a German!

But another Europe exists alongside this one. It is the Europe that fought the Juppé Plan of welfare cuts in France in the mid 1990s; that marched in its millions in all our major cities – London included; the Europe that confronts the G8; that has shouted and sung out its "one no and many yeses" in Prague, London, Paris, Florence, Geneva, Oslo and in just about every town and city in the continent. These are the European heirs of Britain's miners who fought Thatcherism in its infancy.

Kevin P Creighan

Trade unionist, president of the Association of Flight Attendants

As a transplanted American elected as a general secretary to a small trade union in the UK, I'm not sure my views are worthy of note.

Anyway, I feel many in this country are just afraid of the EU. Those who support further integration are afraid to tell the people about the downsides to the EU; those opposing it are afraid it will destroy British rights as a nation. Neither seems based on much rational understanding. So many are afraid of the Euro. The biggest difference it will make is to create uniformity with all the nations we visit so often.

Why are they afraid of immigration from the EU? It's all so emotional. On the right, you would expect they would be happy to see people come in to put downward pressure on wages. On the Left, you would think we would be happy to get additional workers to help expand employment and because it is just the right thing to do.

And European Directives – they're so afraid they create additional red tape, but most of the regulation creates more holiday, more time off, more fair treatment, more safe work places, etc. No, these aren't free, but what's the problem?

If there is anything to fear, it is our collective linguistic inabilities. When I'm at meetings or conferences on the continent, it is only my British colleagues and me who know no other languages. Everyone else is conversing in two, three, or more.

But, none of these fears has a lot to do with reality. They only get in the way of objective analysis of change. Bottom line, change is difficult, and many avoid contemplating change by being afraid and indecisive – not a good thing when contemplating the direction of a country's future.

Will this help in the debate on further integration of the UK into the EU? Probably not. If it helps someone realise the petty fears, that's OK.

Alan Simpson
Labour MP for Nottingham North, socialist and ecologist

Another Europe

Some of the celebrations following France's rejection of the EU Constitution were amazing. Crowd scenes of people singing the 'Internationale' certainly helped dispel the myth that this was just a fit of pique or a retreat into narrow nationalism. I doubt, though, that even the most fervent of celebrants realised that they were re-setting the agenda, not just for Europe, but for the G8 and beyond.

Europe stands at a crossroads. Many of the presumptions that brought Europe's nations together still hold good, but the structures and priorities of today's EU simply do not work. On this, both the Left and the Right probably agree, but it is here that the coalitions of convenience have to part company. A new agenda is needed from the Left that addresses the crises of the current century rather than the insecurities of the last.

France and Germany were right to have looked for ways of linking Europe together in ways that reduced the risk of future wars. But the EU has now become its own Maginot Line. Institutionally sterile, politically unaccountable, the EU has also become the handmaiden to corporate interests rather than of citizens. It is now the sanctuary for a narrow elite while another war rages all around it. This is the war against the poor and the war against the planet.

At the G8 summit in Edinburgh, great play was made of small gestures towards the poor. But the war goes on, and its causes go largely unchallenged. Only outside the gates of summits will you see evidence of a broader social movement that demands change on a different scale. Thirty billion dollars of debt cancellation is not to be sniffed at, but at best it will cancel just $2 billion of debts a year, to the poorest of the poor, when twenty times this amount is needed to have any real impact. Saddest of all is the conditionality attached to the gesture. World leaders talk of 'good governance' when all they mean is privatisation.

'Corruption in Africa' will be the pretext for insisting that its future can only be safe in the hands of the men from Parmalat, Enron, Worldcom, and Monsanto. These are the guys who really know how to fix a deal, build an empire, buy a government. They will show African nations how to set up a sophisticated network of offshore accounting rather than just stuffing cash into suitcases. They are the guys already showing how a new era of imperial conquest and occupation can be brought in by privatisation and patent rather than by the sword and the cross.

As we found out in Iraq, however, if countries are resistant to the market demands of corporate feudalism, the big powers who act as its political agents are not averse to going back to the sword and the cross. Although they argue that this is the last resort, the reality is that today's market fundamentalisms increasingly have to be enforced by repressive state power.

Water and energy privatisations in Latin America trebled prices and caused civil riots as they succeeded in making the poor poorer and the poorest destitute. In Tanzania, they cancelled the water privatisation contract because water was becoming undrinkable. Elsewhere, global corporations have insisted on private security systems to protect their exploitation rights in occupied territories.

These are the human faces of today's free-for-all confusion. The environmental face is arguably much worse. It takes longer for the planet to kick back against abuse but, when it does, the consequences will chase the rich as much as they will chase the poor. This is where a new agenda for Europe must begin.

We are heading towards unavoidable crises of food security, water management and energy supply. Globalisation is accelerating the problem by promoting high product-miles and intensive demands of both energy and water consumption. It is a recipe for resource depletion

(North and South) and for tidal movements of people that follow when exhaustion and pollution overtake production.

The issue in Europe is not food subsidies per se. It is the use of such subsidies to promote over-production in Europe and food-dumping in the developing world. Globally, we have to develop food policies that promote food security (and sustainability) rather than production for global markets.

Energy markets have to be turned around on new market rules; promoting sustainable and renewable energy systems, requiring buildings to generate their own energy rather than just consume it, and looking to conserve as much as we consume.

All across Europe we are counting the cost of serious lurches in weather patterns. The heat wave of 2003 accounted for over 20,000 deaths. Severe flooding in Italy cut river courses into fields not flooded in centuries. In Spain, half of the country is already in drought. And in the UK, areas that were caught up in winter flash flooding are now being warned of summer water shortages.

Europe must harvest a coalition of national interests in conserving the resources we have and using them to promote long term security. Of course there need to be pan-european policies (and the taxation / redistribution mechanisms that support them) but they have to be on a completely different basis.

Britain has just been told that all of the carbon reduction savings we have made in recent years have been more than replaced by increased carbon emissions from aviation. Every government you mention this to merely raises their hands and shrugs. "We cannot tax aviation fuel," they say, "because the trade would all go to other European airports. Our country would lose out."

The compelling case is for EU-wide aviation fuel duties, with the revenue used to fund carbon reduction programmes within member states. Heavier tariff rates could apply to non-EU members, unless they could demonstrate that they had their own similar tariff system. In this case, all revenues could be earmarked for sustainable carbon reduction programmes in the developing world.

Tangential though it may be for Britain, this approach is central to the future of the euro. In or out of the euro, Britain has an interest in social cohesion and growth in the euro zone. The current remit for the central bank is solely about monetary stability. It has thrown much of the EU into recessionary economics. No wonder countries are beginning to debate leaving the euro and 'getting their own currency back.'

The central issue, however, is not the currency but the banking and economic policies behind it. Europe needs to promote full employment, social cohesion and environmental stability; replacing the current obsession with market deregulation and public sector cuts.

Then, there is the issue of the EU budget itself. Britain's rebate is indefensible, but so too is the formula for budget distribution. We need to be honest. With or without a fall-out between Britain and France, not a single member State would increase their EU budget contribution. As new member states acquire full economic rights (post 2012), today's budget arrangements will collapse. This will come at the same time as the insurance industry warns that environmental damage costs will start to spiral. We need another plan.

I have spent the last couple of years exploring this. The alternatives are frighteningly deliverable. The only fear is in abandoning today's free-market deities. We have probably reached the end of multinational, corporate solutions to global problems.

Just as the nuclear industry represents itself as the answer to carbon emissions, London is working on plans to become self-sufficient in renewable energy. The plans would also move into non-toxic waste-recycling, stepping into the hydrogen and fuel cell economy and using heating (and cooling) systems where the by-product is pure water. Much of this work has already been pioneered in Woking and is almost certain to be shared on a global basis. If there is a 21st century 'gift' to be offered to the developing world, this is it.

Amusingly, it would take Britain back to its own origins of energy and lighting policies. At the turn of the last century, municipal authorities had set up their own gas, water and electricity companies to provide security for local citizens. Eventually, these companies were absorbed into the wider systems of either a national grid or big energy supplier.

Today, we know that such suppliers are incredibly inefficient. Local generating systems can deliver energy at around one fifth of the cost of central power stations. All of this can come from sustainable and renewable sources. Nuclear doesn't even enter the equation.

Translate such an approach into jobs and you have a huge new employment infrastructure that sees everything we build – from streetlights to school buildings – as the source of their own energy. It is an approach in which food systems tread lightly on the land that supports them; a mindset in which waste itself becomes a renewable source of water, compost and energy.

All this is happening now. It is what will replace today's confusion of greed and exploitation. It is an answer as much to the confusion of the first world as to the poverty of the third world. Not a sliver of this will be understood or articulated within the G8. It is an agenda waiting to take shape outside. This is why we must shape it ourselves.

Vicky Tuck
Principal, Cheltenham Ladies College

I have just returned from a short trip to Alsace whose capital, Strasbourg is, as you know, home to the European Parliament. I am well aware of the cynicism about the lifestyle of MEPs enjoying the culinary and oenological delights of this fertile region but I am also conscious of the great weight of Alsace's history and feel that we should not lose sight of the impressive achievement of the EU in preserving peace in Western Europe for half a century. Of course the challenges before the EU today with 27 member states and its largest, Germany, still overcoming the impact of reunification, are considerable. Of course there is much that is imperfect, but I feel firmly rooted in our European heritage, especially as a linguist.

I have spent time in recent years in Asia and have witnessed the dynamism and entrepreneurial spirit of the East. Europe will struggle to compete with this growth but it should remember what the Chinese, Singaporeans and Malaysians understand so well – that economic prosperity is dependent on education, creativity and a strong work ethic. I don't think the quality of education and the investment in education are sufficient in many parts of Europe, including the UK. The EU's infrastructure and its legislative framework, for all their strengths, will not safeguard political and social harmony if there is widespread unemployment and disaffection.

Penny Rimbaud

Novelist, performance poet, social commentator and founder of punk band 'Crass'

Treasure Island

That Britain is a member of the EU, and therefore a part of Europe, is a fact which appears to be beyond the grasp of some of the British and most of the English. Perhaps because Britain under the governance of England is itself divided into four nations, it is impossible for the English State to accept any rule but its own; clinging to its imperialist past, of which Ireland, Scotland and Wales were the first victims, it appears afraid to countenance mainland Europe, lest in some way its deluded idea of supremacy be challenged. UK rules OK? Well, not quite.

Back in the 1980s, in reaction to Britain's and her own fast-sinking world status, Margaret Thatcher opted for the fierce individualism of the American Right. Having smelted her iron through a personal war with the Falklands, for which the British people were ordered to 'rejoice', she then set about the miners, tearing apart tight-knit working-class communities while without a hint of irony declaring, "There is no such thing as society." By so thoroughly demeaning long-standing traditions of pride and dignity (while at the same time making way for ersatz New Labour), her abandonment of Britain to 'super size me' America was complete. Having thus single-handedly stripped the nation of whatever cultural and ancestral roots it might once have possessed both at home and in mainland Europe, Thatcher then retreated to the star-spangled boudoir of her pre-senile political paramour, Ronald Reagan.

However, despite having suffered centuries of cultural oppression, the Irish, the Scots and the Welsh were not impressed. Having managed against all odds to retain some quality of national integrity, they still possessed the sense of community so derided by Thatcher, yet so essential to any nation looking towards a united Europe. In the (dis)United Kingdom of Great Britain, it was England that had traditionally called the shots, but in the contemporary world of Europe it was way off target.

Whereas the English language spoken in Britain once shared ideological roots with the Europe, English as spoken in America shares none. Today, endlessly bombarded with American capitalist propaganda, yet having origins in the more socialistic thought of Europe, the English suffer from a profound cultural schizophrenia. Torn between two conflicting world-views, they quite simply don't know whether they are coming or going. Nonetheless, for all this, they treasure their island; the 'English Channel' being as effective a cultural barrier as was once the Berlin Wall. But that works both ways; ideologically removed from America and Europe, the English are, whether they like it or not, an island unto themselves. Equally, having so wholeheartedly embraced free-market capitalism, England has thrown itself like a two-faced clown into an impossible cul-de-sac where, through having no interests but its own, it is in no position to consider genuine union with Europe: in other words, "Sod the Union Jack, where's me Cross of Saint George?"

Putting aside the possibly sinister implications of a single currency and a combined army (economic and military interests being incorrigible bed-partners), the concept of a Europe without frontiers is as much anathema to the English State as any idea of 'externally' imposed human rights. While remaining passively leashed to America, the English State vigorously asserts its separateness from Europe so that it may hang on to its deluded sense of world power and at the same time continue in its very real oppression of the citizens of Britain. While the English State takes the moral high-ground on global matters, it blatantly ignores issues closer to home: beneath the glare of its crusade in Iraq, the occupation of Northern Ireland has been all but forgotten, yet it continues unabashed. For as long as the English State is free in the guise of democracy to oppress the occupied nations of Britain, so it will resist the more genuinely democratic policies of the EU. Belonging yet not belonging, England's relationship with Europe shows in truth a closer affinity to Alice's Wonderland than it does to any ideal of modern-day diplomacy: more tea?

Being by nature xenophobic (even towards their fellow Britons), the English are incapable of embracing a truly unified Europe. It was, after all, their favourite statesman, Winston Churchill (he who invented concentration camps and was first to bomb the Kurds), who once proclaimed that "Wops begin at Calais", a sentiment repeated time and time again by those whose opposed the Channel Tunnel because it destroyed England's natural defensive barrier against Europe (and its "wops"). Caught up in a double-bind of their own making, the English are historically and culturally a part of Europe, yet at the same time remain stolidly apart from it. Supported by Murdoch's bile-ridden press, they will doggedly continue to proclaim their isolationism through not so thinly veiled Churchillian racism, while the English State, imperialist to the bitter end, will resolutely pay no more than lip-service to the EU.

In its resistance to a changing Europe, England has proved itself to be the nation of small-minded shopkeepers that Napoleon in his Gallic wisdom knew it to be. It is not a question of whether or not England should wholeheartedly embrace Europe, as much as should Europe accept in its midst a nation whose only contribution to date has been its mean-spiritedness? Having abandoned socialistic ideals in favour of rampant capitalism, and showing no real willingness to recognise the genuine demands of Northern Ireland, Scotland and Wales, there is clearly no place for England in Europe. While the rest of Europe is attempting to play the game to EU rules, the English will continue to stamp their feet insisting that it's "simply not cricket." When Charles De Gaulle attempted to block Britain's entry into the Common Market, he knew exactly what he was doing: why allow an inveterate, unrepentant bully into your playground?

Waiting for the trump card to be shown, the English State hops uncomfortably between the conflicting ideologies of Europe and America. Should America fail in its bid for global domination, the English will be calling post-haste on the battered boats of Dunkirk to take them across ‘their’ Channel to the golden gates of Europe. On the other hand, for as long as the English State can get by on the dog-ends of its ‘special relationship’ with the New World and its Order, there will be very little chance of anything more than token union with Europe, and bugger the smelly cheese.

Simon Buckby
Founding director of Britain in Europe, currently working as a media consultant

Britain & Europe: Where Next?

After years of gradual retreat, Britain's pro-Europeans are now on the run. We have long been hunted down by a hysterical anti-European media fed by populist politicians and campaigners that are only too happy to twist the truth to undermine public confidence that the European Union can serve Britain's national interests. Now it appears we have even been more or less abandoned by a government that once proudly proclaimed it an urgent priority to face down anti-European scaremongering but has ended up shouting at our Continental partners in a way that Margaret Thatcher would have been proud of. It really can't get any worse than this, can it?

The no votes on the proposed constitution in France and the Netherlands have created a defining moment in Europe's post-war history. They are not mere blips. They cannot be ignored. They need to be understood – by all sides.

These votes certainly do not amount to a rejection of the current principles of the European Union. If anything, apart from the discreet national issues at stake in each case, they represented a blow to the free trade model frequently touted by anti-Europeans here in Britain, which is feared on the Continent as a likely assault on their system of welfare capitalism. However, these votes should be seen as a decisive demand by the people of Europe to call their political leaders to account, to tell them to stop hurrying along with grand projects of infrastructure and architecture, and instead to return to managing the real issues of economic reform and social support. Above all, these votes should be heard loud and clear as an instruction for Europe's elites not to leave their publics behind, but to nurture constantly their consent for every development in the complex process of building an essential European co-operation.

The immediate fallout of these no votes has been appallingly damaging for the national interests of all concerned as well as for the stability of Europe as a whole. Relieved he did not have to hold a referendum he almost certainly would have lost, Tony Blair sought to blame the French for toppling the constitution. Retorting that he would never have called a referendum in the first place had Blair not done so, Jacques Chirac focussed his anger on Britain.

This battle was then waged via the proxy issue of Britain's overblown budget rebate versus the French farmers' too big a claim on the Common Agricultural Policy; rarely has such un-diplomatic language been screamed across the Channel. Both sides are sure of their tactics – to make sure it's all seen to be the other's fault – while strategy has been abandoned – neither knows where they are going or where they want to take Europe.

Germany has been out of the picture, so at this moment of crisis Europe's biggest three, the traditional power balancers, have been unable to provide any cohesive leadership. If this situation continues, there is a very grave danger that in the long term Europe could descend into stagnation, as in the 1970s, or worse it could even fragment, surely unimaginable so soon after the launch of the single currency and membership enlargement to the east.

So, what is to be done?

First and foremost, Europe's leaders need to reconnect the project of European cooperation with the interests and aspirations of Europe's peoples. By leaving their electorates behind, the elites have fostered at best apathy and at worst – as in the no votes and in the hysteria found in parts of the British press – resentment of what they are up to. The new slogan for our era should be simple: no more grand projects; stick to the issues that matter to people please. Hence there is now a huge task for politicians to remind their voters why and how European cooperation can help further the interests of their nations in a variety of crucial policy areas.

None of these areas is more important than the economy, stupid. With Europe's long term growth rates consistently below those of the United States, with pockets of severe unemployment and with the impact of the single currency on monetary policy becoming more obvious, Europe needs structural reform to become more flexible and more competitive. Yet contrary to the impression often given over the years by British ministers in Europe, there is no off-the-shelf package of measures that can simply be imposed on all parts of the Continent, from Germany to Poland. Instead, Europe needs to be guided towards economic reform by a mature leadership, not from the Commission but from the principal national governments, who instinctively understand the need to search for an inclusive consensus.

Britain, of course, continues to be well placed to provide this leadership. With France and Germany no longer the dominant duopoly of old, there is room for a serious third force. Moreover, we have the credibility that comes from running one of the best performing economies. However, we also, of course, continue to be held back in this task by a political culture and a media environment that demands our ministers go to fight for Blighty in the negotiating halls of the Berlaymont as if they were the battlefields of the Somme. We will not lead a consensus for reform through a hectoring style that simply exhorts others to do to their economies what we have done to ours. We will only lead by understanding and encouraging the interests of others.

For there is the nub of the European Union's founding principles and the core of the schism in British politics. European cooperation is not a zero sum game: each nation is stronger in the EU only when we are all stronger, and therefore we need not fight to do others down. That is the point of pooling some of our national sovereignty in specific areas. It is the failure of British pro-Europeans to win this argument here that has left the centre of gravity of debate about Britain in Europe so far removed from the facts of life. Until that changes, our ministers will never feel sufficiently free to make the necessary big picture arguments to lead in Europe because they will always be watching their backs at home.

The kind of leadership that Europe needs and Britain ought to supply requires an elevated appreciation of our national interests – one that has been sadly lacking in this country for more than a generation. It demands that the prime minister explain to people what he is doing and why. Otherwise they will, in truth, have no de facto mandate for such a leadership role.

I am fed up and embarrassed that every few months I publicly claim that such and such an event might just trigger the long-heralded start of a government-led pro-European campaign. Yet even this government, who declared for itself right at the beginning the need to win again the case for Britain in Europe, has never missed an opportunity to miss an opportunity. Well, never mind: perhaps, just perhaps, without the hysteria attached to an imminent referendum, the case for Britain in Europe can be made (and contested) rather more soberly than in the recent past. Only in this way can Britain have the space to perform the leadership function that Europe so badly needs.

Geoffrey Burgon

Composer

I do not feel like a European, but culturally I do feel part of Europe. As a composer I would have to say that European music taken as a whole has influenced me much more than British music. I would probably have gone to study in Europe after leaving music school if family commitments hadn't prevented me. Whether that would have ultimately made my work sound any different in the long term is impossible to say, although it might well have accelerated my development as a composer. But not hearing European music at all would have been a huge loss, and inevitably have led to my work remaining parochial.

In the 60s, when I was at music school in London, the influence of Europe was not so positive for me and a lot of other composers. The contemporary music establishment in Britain was heavily biased towards the post-Second Viennese School, exemplified by Stockhausen and Boulez. The latter was conducting the BBC Symphony Orchestra and had a dominant influence over what was performed. William Glock was head of music at the BBC and was of the same aesthetic persuasion as Boulez, as were most of the music staff at Broadcasting House. If composers didn't write in a language that they approved of (and I was one of them) they were beyond the pale. As a result, a lot of the music that was written and performed at that time was in a rather bland, anonymous style, a kind of Euro-sound, most of which is now forgotten. I think that the musical establishment here was afraid that 'Englishness' meant parochialism. There was some justification for this. The generation of composers that Vaughan Williams influenced were still producing music that suggested that they were unaware of the existence of Stravinsky, Webern and Bartok. Most of this work was very insipid and second rate. Understandably Boulez, for instance, would never programme it. But he was also very reluctant to perform Benjamin Britten's work too, regarding him as a reactionary of the same ilk. Yet most serious music lovers regarded Britten as one of the greatest voices in contemporary music, and certainly the most important British composer since Elgar.

The reaction to this European dominance began in the USA, with Philip Glass, Terry Riley and, a little later, John Adams. Theirs was a direct reaction to the musical culture of Europe. They wanted a freer, more rhythmically dynamic music and this led to minimalism. Of course there was a whole other thing happening in pop music, and at first the minimalists found their audience there rather than in the 'serious' music culture. Their influence eventually found its way to Europe and Great Britain. Gradually the 'Euro-music' of the 60s became marginalised, as minimalism and a more neo-romantic music began to be programmed, and composers of all persuasion began to have their works played again.

Perhaps one has to embrace European culture in order to discover one's own national qualities, as in the Chinese proverb 'You have to travel in order to discover that you needn't have left home in the first place'. James Joyce, for instance, exiled himself from his native Ireland then spent the rest of his life writing about it, apparently not influenced by European literature at all. On the other hand Stravinsky, after the early very Russian-influenced ballets, embraced European music, although it's debatable whether he affected it more than it affected him.

I wonder how 'European' the average French, German or an Italian person feels, as opposed to thinks? My guess is not very. Take cars. Can you imagine the Italians producing a Volvo, or the Swedes a Ferrari? And I can't imagine anyone but the British making the Bristol 405 Drop Head Convertible. This may seem flippant, but I think it indicates as well as anything that national characteristics exist and always will, and calling ourselves European is unlikely to change that.

I can see the point of a free trade agreement with Europe, but we don't seem to have free trade. I can see the political (and military) pragmatism of a united Europe, as a 'force' to oppose the power of the

USA and, in the future, perhaps China. But, whilst I feel that we are inextricably linked culturally, whether economic and political links will ever make any of us feel more European than national remains to be seen.

Freya Juppy
Photographer

Continental Cleft

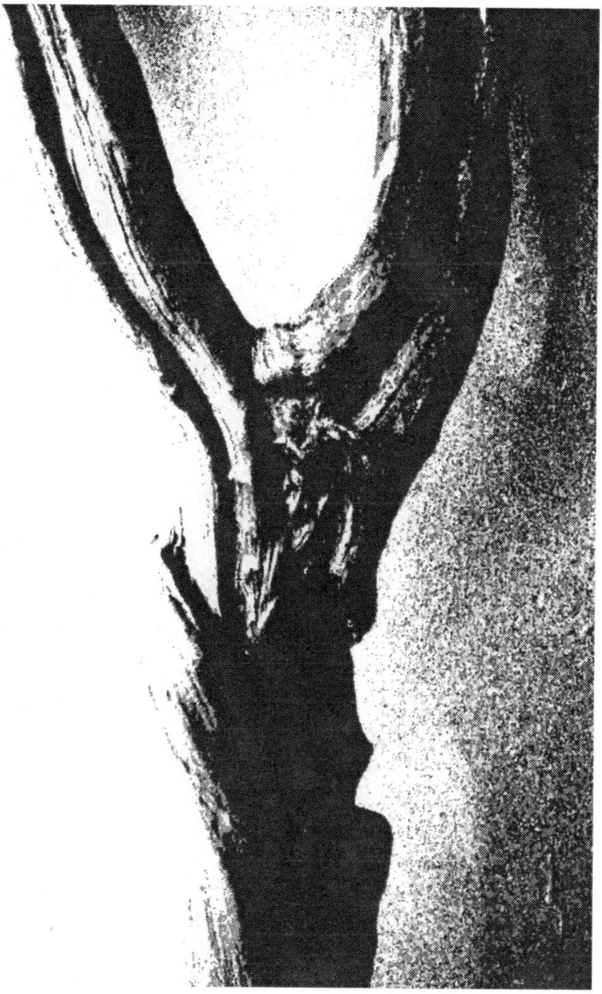

John Dallat

Member of the Northern Ireland Assembly (East Derry) for the Social, Democratic and Labour Party (SDLP)

It was only after the dreadful events of the September 11th 2001 terrorist attacks in New York, Washington and Philadelphia that America's best kept secret got out – only ten percent of Americans have passports. The percentage of people in Britain and Ireland carrying passports is much higher but how much of that has to do with the enlargement of the European Union? I suggest a great deal and I further forecast that the benefits of enlargement will make a major contribution to our economy at home and to the development of the economies of those countries which have either just joined or are in the process of doing so.

As an individual with no real history of travel I could never have envisaged visiting Slovenia, for example. Yet recently, thanks to low-cost air travel, I was able to book an Easy Jet flight from Belfast to Stanstead, wait a short time and board another Easy Jet flight to the capital of that beautiful country, Ljubljana. As a politician it was necessary for me to see what has been achieved since Slovenia achieved independence 11 years ago and how excited the people are at becoming the newest member of the European Union.

Most of my neighbours have been to Prague and have returned bewildered with the sheer splendour of that city, the hospitality of its people and the depth of its history. I suggest that neither of these two examples I have chosen would have been possible for the vast majority of people without the expansion of the European Union which has created a fascination with those countries cut off behind the Iron

Curtain for so long. It seemed that the time warp imposed on travel had suddenly been lifted and life is beginning where it left off so many years ago.

Back at home I now enjoy going to Lidl Stores as a cultural experience because this group is a recognised chain store group across Europe and has become a honey pot for migrant workers from the enlarged European Union. It is in these stores that I find those people who are now making a significant impact on the development of our economy. Our new found friends from Bulgaria, Romania, Latvia, the Ukraine, Lithuania, Poland, the Czech Republic as well as the older European members, including Portugal in particular, are making an enormous contribution, not just to our economy but to developing a more informed perception of the world beyond our island shores.

The positive side of this new development enabled by the enlargement of the European Union has been lost on some and in particular those who stir up racism. But the positive impact has, I believe, overwhelmed any serious attempt to create strife.

The tragedies are more likely to be felt in other directions and, in particular, the absence of any real safety network for those who find that they have lost their jobs or have unforeseen problems which require the support of the social services freely available to the indigenous population.

Take, for example, the plight of the Ukrainian girl, Oksana Sukhanova, aged 23 who lost her job in a meat factory in Northern Ireland and became homeless because her accommodation went with the job. After sleeping rough over Christmas the poor girl turned up with her former workmates on New Year's Day suffering from severe frostbite. Both her legs have been amputated to save her life and, as I write, she is recovering in a Belfast hospital. We are not sure if her parents know of her ordeal. Oksana has paid a terrible price for the benefits we all enjoy of an enlarged Europe and, while we can't put the clock back and restore her limbs, we can at least learn that there are also responsibilities for the benefits we receive from the free movement of labour in an enlarged European Union.

Ironically, while this dreadful news was breaking, two of the three MEPs from Northern Ireland were voting against the new European Constitution which is, in reality, a simplification of the previous indigestible maze of treaties and amendments to make things clearer and more transparent for the lay person.

Obviously the European Union is no longer just a regulated market but an arena for democratic politics which has replaced the cold war divide and has made a major contribution to levering up democratic standards in those parts of the world which were previously behind the Iron Curtain.

For me both as an individual and a politician it has been an exciting time which until this week has explored nothing but the positives. Now my mind is firmly fixed on the tragedy of that Ukranian girl Oksana Sukhanova and the price she has paid for the enormous benefits flowing from an enlarged European Union. Let us hope that her suffering and pain is not lost and new practices will come into being which provide a much-needed safety net she didn't have.

I am encouraged by a lady living close to Oksana's former work colleagues who is brushing up her Russian so that she can be of help to those who live in her neighbourhood hailing from the Ukraine – Oksana's native country. After all, it is a two-way process and we should realise that.

Tony Little
Headmaster of Eton College

When I was 18, back-packing around Europe was a challenge, a voyage of personal discovery in strange and different places. For a modern teenage generation, Europe is a backyard of common living where differences are purged; fine for a family holiday – but an exciting world of the new? First stop, Bali.

For some, this stepping stone on the path to globalisation is sure and good: it is the destiny of man to evolve from primitive insularity to parochial understanding to global reason. What need of the trivial differences that have separated men and led to misunderstanding, confusion, bitterness and war? Who would wish for a Tower of Babel?

When I speak with young people about Europe, they see virtue in shared values and aspirations, in the desire to live and work co-operatively, forging a future without feeling shackled to the past. But institutions which they perceive to function largely as procedural and managerial entities and which strip away cultural richness and moral debate and instead impose more rules, they see as reducing and limiting their lives. There is a beauty and dignity in recognising and celebrating our differentness. Europe? Vive la difference!

Michael Bell
Professor Emeritus at the University of Warwick and Fellow of the British Academy

Personal Reflections on the Meaning of Europe

It looks to me as if Europe has a meaning to many of my generation that it has ceased to have for our children.

I was born in 1941, conceived in the time of the Blitz. Although brought up in England, I was mainly Irish a generation or so back and in mature years this began to explain to me the irredeemable strangeness of the English as a club to which I did not belong. Being brought up Catholic, on the other hand, gives you a sense of belonging to an international world. I can recollect no encounter with racial prejudice in my youth: the world was divided into Catholics and non-Catholics while all other distinctions were relatively unimportant. Almost all my early encounters with foreigners were in one way or another through the Church and something of this formation lingers long after any adherence to a religious faith.

My parents were intelligent working-class of the generation that left school at fourteen and had no liberal education but they had a natural disdain for the commercialised culture aimed at the working class. They worked hard for their children, all four of whom went to grammar schools and became formally middle class. This external fact can have different personal meanings, however. Growing up solidly within a class gives a sense of security even if you subsequently move, indeed it makes it possible to move, but I think it is rarely realised how damaging it can be to have your formative years between classes so that every gesture and accent is at every moment suddenly and mysteriously subject to ridicule. At the age of fifteen I went on an exchange to a family in Millau, in the south of France, and that was when I became aware of a wider world in which I was not so strange after all. Or rather perhaps, I was strange but the world around me was not.

On completing a degree at London in English Literature, I spent a year in Lyon, France, as an English Assistant in a school. My catholic grammar school, only just promoted from being a private fee-paying college for boys who had failed the scholarship, or 11 plus, had been very limited intellectually and in its range. It had no Greek, German, biology or chemistry in my time. In France, I encountered students from Germany and wanted to learn the language. I came back, spent a year teaching, and then went to Germany for a year as a language assistant and read as much as I could. The next year I found myself, at short notice through a personal connection, in a junior academic post in Canada where I started a university career. I stayed for five years while presenting an external PhD at London. This was on the most English of authors, DH Lawrence, but arguing in effect that he is best understood through a German tradition of thought.

After completing the thesis I taught for three years in upstate New York. The displacement to North America, especially if one is not intending to stay, gives a strong new sense of being European. When you meet a Frenchman there, it is with the odd sense of meeting a countryman. Although I enjoyed life in America, it always had a relative thinness to me, the obverse of its free and open horizon, and I kept an underlying homesickness, not for Britain, but for Europe.

The relations between German, French and English modes of thought and being have remained an important focus for the rest of my life. Although each is complete in its way, each needs the others to make it properly self-conscious, to allow one to see its human proportions, strengths and limitations. At a younger age, abroad represented an escape from the tiresome miasma of class; the world where even genuine values have a class appropriation. As one got beyond that to start understanding the values in themselves, the major European cultures were inescapably part of one's being. But that is where the generational question comes in. My children's generation seem to have little, if any, such feeling about Europe, and students are increasingly less concerned to invest in the European languages and cultures. They have grown up with the EU and take Europe for granted as their home region so that the foreign starts, or becomes interesting, only in other continents. Of course, that does not mean they like Europe, any more than the more demanding of the English have found their countrymen entirely likeable or admirable. It just refers to the focus of interest, and they may well be right in their generation. They will be living in a crowded planet with instant global connections and full of dangerous frictions. The shift seems to involve a loss of the *Innigkeit* that is associated with reflection on the powers of language, and the romance of etymology, which was so powerful for thoughtful people of my generation. But that may be precisely the baggage that must be dropped.

I was struck by the recent remark of a new young colleague, of German Jewish origin brought up in New York, who was taking British citizenship at one of the new ceremonies instituted under David Blunkett. My colleague, who is deeply unhappy with American foreign policies, took the matter of citizenship very seriously but would have been happy to take out a European citizenship, had it been available. It would be interesting to know how many people, native and immigrant, might wish to have European citizenship, whether in addition to, or instead of, a national one. I can certainly understand such a feeling. National citizenship is currently the only last resort guarantee of some personal rights but it may not correspond with the personal identifications of all citizens. Politically speaking, the EU is in itself a troubling and unlovely institution and it may be that an organisation of its size is necessarily beyond control. Nonetheless, in the globalised world, it is going to be a necessary evil with which we must do the best we can and psychologically and culturally I don't mind throwing in my lot with other Europeans.

Ian O Angell
Professor of information systems, London School of Economics

The impact of ICT on Britain and the EU or What do you get when you mix the British Pound (B£) with the EURO?

According to the OECD's latest report there is a clear relationship between Information and Communication Technologies (ICT) and economic growth. However, it goes on to show that success is not in the technology itself, rather in the organisational and institutional (political and cultural) structures surrounding the application of new technology, and whether those structures are predisposed to take advantage. ICT, together with speedy international travel, is ushering in whole new ways of doing business. Telecoms networks, covering the globe via cable and satellite, enable everyone in the world (at least those who can afford it) to 'talk' to, and to trade with everyone else. Anyone bypassed faces ruin. Even with technology, countries, companies, currencies can still lose out.

Before considering the effect of ICT on Britain and/or the EU, we should start by considering the ICT-rich company of the future, and what it will look like. Nobel prizewinner Ronald Coase gave us a hint over 60 years ago. He asked the fundamental question: 'why do firms exist at all?' Why do entrepreneurs and workers group together in a firm, rather than buy and sell each other's services on the open market? The deciding factor he said is transaction costs: the costs incurred in the development of commercial contracts. Each firm is formed when it is cheaper to organise as a group, rather than buy and sell contracts in the marketplace.

But, and it is a big but, the firm will stop growing when those goods and services can be purchased more cheaply in the marketplace. This idea is dynamite for the Information Age. It explains much of the turmoil we feel today. For now 'spot markets' are forming in cyberspace. ICT, the Internet, linked with advanced manufacturing technologies, international travel and transport, has changed fundamentally the nature of transactions, and hence their costs. The structure of yesterday's company was an answer to the question: 'what is a viable firm?' against the judgments of the transaction costs from the Industrial Age. Today, the answers to this same question is delivering a radically different animal.

The dominant hierarchical and bureaucratic firm has passed its sell-by date. This juggernaut of the factory metaphor, that won the battles of natural selection during the Industrial Age, is being totally out-manoeuvred by different organisational forms that are emerging. Companies are setting themselves up within 'virtual enterprises,' at the hub of loosely knit alliances – *joint ventures* linked together by global networks: electronic, transport and particularly human. They assemble to take advantage of any temporary business opportunity; and then separate, each company moving on to its next major deal.

Each virtual enterprise is project-based, and developed around complex information systems: the information system *is* the virtual enterprise; there is nothing else. It *is* the headquarters; and it can be based *virtually* anywhere in 'Cyberspace'. However, you can forget all the hyperbole: e-business is just business. The business case is self-evident. By forging electronic links in the supply and value chains, firms can radically reduce the paper-chase of invoicing etc. This means big savings, not only by making the back office far more efficient, but also by substantially reducing the number of paper-chasers – *by firing people!* How will the institutions in the EU and the UK react to losing the jobs made unnecessary by ICT? And it's not only semi-skilled jobs. In the latest recessional bloodletting in the City of London, almost a third of jobs have gone, but unlike previous recessions it is unlikely (because of the functionality of ICT) that many will return with the return of better times.

For the past two decades we have witnessed the Solow paradox. Although huge sums were spent on Office Automation, there was no increase in efficiency. And why not? The office was treated as a stand-alone entity, rather than as a single node in a network of partner organisations, which managed the value and supply chains. With the arrival of the generic Internet technology, the office can be integrated into the overall network, and huge savings can be made from the synergy found among partner organisations, and by leveraging the effectiveness of systems across the network.

Using new technology, firms are redefining totally the very 'nature of work'. The job for life, an idea from the Machine Age, has gone. During the economic recovery of 1992–1996, less than a third of the jobs created in Britain were full time. The Henley Centre predicts that by 2010 less than half of all jobs will be full time. Using the networked portable computer and the ubiquitous mobile phone, firms are turning office workers into 'teleworkers', and squeezing 30 percent more work out of them. Yesterday's office workers sat next to a unique telephone number and a filing cabinet stuffed with paper. Now they are 'road warriors,' taking their phone numbers and files with them, anywhere. Company functions are being outsourced to freelancers, on a 'pay-as-you-need' basis. A new type of worker is appearing, the 'self-employed portfolio worker', working for a number of different companies, and based at home, being paid (poorly) on piece-rate.

There will be far more flexible employment (a euphemism for part-time and casual work). Even today, one in eight UK workers is self-employed. The top US employer is not General Electric or General Motors, but Manpower, the 'temping' agency, with over three-quarters of a million 'temps' on its books. How will European work practices cope with such pressures?

We don't know what a job is any more. According to Peter Drucker, humanity is polarising into two employment categories: the intellectual, cultural and business elite (the mobile and independent *knowledge workers*) – the *alphas*; and the rest (the immobile and dependent *service workers*). Drucker himself dislikes the term knowledge worker, because he is clear that the real issue is 'talent' and not 'knowledge'. For paradoxically, only talent can leverage the added value from this technology. One thing never changes: the need for *innovation* and *talent*.

Sixty years ago Joseph Schumpeter explained growth in terms of a rush of technological innovation unleashing competition between firms, thereby creating an upsurge in investment and new industries. The mediocre do not lead innovation – they follow it! Nor does capital investment by itself create growth. It is the innovators, not the investors, that create jobs and generate wealth. An arbitrary investment in training the 'workforce,' a legion of second-raters, or investment in an educational infrastructure and capital equipment, can all lead to waste. Without an investment in elite knowledge workers, countries will fall into a vicious circle of decline. It is the individual innovator who ultimately generates wealth. Hence labour and talent must no be longer treated under one heading. Individuals are *not* standardised units. Talent, the great divider of humanity, must be seen as the diviner of economic success. It is in short supply, and so is in great demand. How will institutions (in both the UK and EU), born in the century of the masses, react to such an individualistic world?

No company/country can succeed without a talented workforce, and so talent work must either go to where talent workers are located, or these alphas must be seduced away. The umbilical cords have been cut; global companies no longer feel the need to support the national aspirations of the countries of their birth. They walk away from a country just as easily as they enter it. Thomas Jefferson recognised this truth over two hundred years ago: "merchants have no country. The mere spot where they stand on does not constitute so strong an attachment as that from which they draw their gain." Successful enterprises are indifferent to, and unhindered by, national boundaries and barriers. The company of the future is transnational, and it will relocate (physically, fiscally and electronically) to where the profit is greatest and the regulation least. Now companies think globally, because they can communicate globally and because the shareholders, the executive, and the employees are spread out across the globe!

The tension between organisational and institutional pressures is coming to a head. If the demands of service workers are excessive then routine office and production will either be replaced by robots, or exported anywhere on the globe: to countries using regulatory arbitrage, less stringent legal requirements, and more advantageous employment and tax regulations to suck in the migrant rich. Britain has already lost

50,000 jobs to the Far East, with an estimate of another 200,000 to go in the next 5 years.

The automation and the exportation of jobs is sending shock waves through western workforces previously protected by national interests, but which are now incapable of fending off foreign incursions. It's tough out there and there is no room for sentimentality in a world where *quality* is far more important than *quantity*. Companies have no choice: they must ask, and answer, some very brutal questions concerning which workers are resources and which are liabilities. They will reduce the wages and staffing levels of service workers, and it is no accident that most are instigating major *downsizing*, *delayering* and *outsourcing* programmes. The structured world of semi-skilled labour, which arose out of the industrial revolution, is disintegrating, and taking with it the political ideologies of collectivism.

The 20th century will be remembered not as a battle between the collectives of the left and right, but as the domination of the individual by the tribe; as the control of trade by collective ideologies. But the 20th century is over. The backward looking idea, that work involves physical effort, no longer convinces. It is that rare commodity, human talent, which is the stuff of work in tomorrow's world. Of course labour is needed – but there is a world full of labourers out there. According to the ILO, nearly a billion sub-employed people have entered the global job market. Labour has become a commodity, and must compete on price.

Companies and countries now see that talent is the real generator of wealth. It always has been, only now the talent workers themselves realise it. The income of these owners of intellectual capital will increase substantially, as they are made welcome anywhere in the world. Both companies and countries must pay a premium to attract talent workers – and to keep them. From October 1994, foreign "entrepreneurial investors" with £1 million at their disposal can bypass the usual entry rules into Britain. Laetitia Casta, the model who, in 2000, posed for the statue of 'Marianne,' the symbol of French womanhood found in town halls all across France, became a tax-exile in London. In the United States, there is a fast-track immigration policy for businessmen and women who can offer $1 million and guarantee to employ ten people. Thousands of millionaires have emigrated to the USA in recent years.

Their H1-B programme hands out six-year visas to 115,000 skilled foreign hi-tech workers every year. Then there's the L2 programme, with no quota. Not surprising: the US has a shortfall of 900,000 hi-tech workers. Furthermore, they are looking for 1.2 million nurses over the next ten years! What are Europe and the UK doing to counter these smash and grab raids on their talent?

Inexorably, the slow redistribution of wealth that has occurred over the last centuries is being reversed, and rapidly. The future, like the past, is inequality. Karl Marx recognised this well over a century ago. Every new technology leads to alienation, and eventually to a polarisation of wealth. The rich get richer, and the poor get poorer. How will British and European institutions react? The intensifying power struggle between the owners of intellectual capital and of financial capital will change fundamentally the very nature of capitalism. The only stable relationship between capital and talent, the only viable model for employment, will be the 'star system' of the sport, entertainment and financial sectors; proto-typical information industries. A few stars earn huge sums of money, the middle is comfortably off, and a large rump of 'wannabes' work part-time on a casual basis, hoping to make the big-time. In a rapidly integrating world economy talent can flee a country, and so will be immune to taxation; in fact these elite wealth generating job creators must be bribed to stay. They must be showered with tax credits, tax holidays and other incentives including reduced regulation. Arbitrage pressures, the exploitation of price, tax and regulation differentials, mean that the end of progressive taxation is in sight.

States must learn that they are now just another form of commercial enterprise frantically trying to find employment for their masses – and they will have to be run like corporations and survive economically on the efforts of an elite few – and no nation-state (and indeed no political unit) has an automatic right to exist. The role of the state is to facilitate an appropriate institutional environment, and to produce the right people, with the right talent and expertise, for the global companies that profit from the Information Age, to service these companies, to provide them with an efficient infrastructure, a minimally regulated market and a secure, stable and comfortable place to operate. The state must nurture, propagate and supply the quality human raw material at the bottom end of the value chain that ultimately creates wealth. This wealth is not the product of labour, but of individual intellect and determination. If a state cannot produce a quality 'people product', then it must buy them from abroad. States will be scouring the globe for elite talent workers, no matter what their age, sex, race or religion. Drag them off the planes if necessary. But nobody wants more service workers, who are increasingly seen as economic liabilities. Hence all anachronistic cultural pressures, so typical of Europe, that interfere with the collection of talent must be dissipated.

Still we hear the rhetoric: government will make Britain, France, the European Union a world power in e-commerce. They incant the abracadabra words 'jobs through growth' and 'training in new technology.' The Lisbon Accord is a case in point: apparently Europe will become a world leader in e-commerce and all things 'e-'. The evidence to date totally denies this rhetoric. Politicians pretend they can conjure up hundreds of thousands of new jobs for the huge number of soon-to-be-unemployed. What a nerve! Businesses create jobs, governments create non-jobs, paid for by taxes. In making non-jobs, they tax real jobs out of existence. In Britain and the EU an army of tax collectors and regulators is abroad – excess regulation is a tax in all but name. The parallel with the Fall of the Rome is there for all to see. That empire was not brought down by barbarians, but by the state bleeding the population white. The Dark Ages were ushered in with the destruction of the Empire's economic viability as a rapacious government seized the wealth of the propertied classes, all in the name of protecting them from external threats, and paying to placate an unruly mob. It sounds just like European democracy!

Governments blithely ignore Coase's warnings at their peril: high transaction costs of centrally-planned economies (including excessive taxation and regulation) inevitably lead to collapse. When will they ever learn that *technology is the problem, not the solution*? Growth is created from the talent of knowledge workers, not from the labour of low-grade service and production workers. National economies can no longer grow themselves out of unemployment. Growth has been decoupled from employment. Productivity is being delivered by a technology needing only a few machine minders. It is clear from Coase's theory that the large number of job losses reported across the Western world is not the result of some temporary downturn in the economic cycle, but is instead the result of structural change.

The really big question that every country has to answer is 'why do some areas become successful hot-spots, while others are doomed to failure?' Which areas are going to win? The answer is amazingly simple; when the area is attractive to talent workers it can win, otherwise it fails. Capital investment by itself does not create wealth. Without an investment in elite talent workers, areas will fall into a vicious circle of decline. Success only comes to dynamic economic hot-spots of innovation and profit.

However, innovation does not happen, just because of a capital investment in scientific and technological research. These deliver mere possibilities. Continuous innovation by the talent worker is the key to success. There are clever people everywhere, so why is prosperity so unevenly distributed? Innovation cannot be banked like capital or stored like a commodity. There can be no plans for innovation, only the initiation of the process. Innovation requires an economic stimulus/catalyst. It happens when science and technology are applied as inventions in a dynamic self-generating economic hot-spot of innovation, investment and profit.

The successful hot-spot will have discovered a balance between social capital and the investment in both physical infrastructure and individual intellectual capital. Spectacular growth comes from these self-perpetuating hot-spots that thrive on their own energy. This energy drives a rapid, almost uncontrolled diffusion of technological techniques and knowledge. The hot-spot itself fuels the engine of endogenous growth by delivering innovation. But only within a network of trust relationships, where only invited talent is allowed to join in an institutional environment that both mobilises the intellectually gifted, and promotes and finances entrepreneurial activity by delivering the right incentives.

In hot-spots, companies will hire start-up companies, trusting in their own judgment of the staff in those new firms. Companies in 'cold-spots' look to trade with firms bearing an 'Established 1800' label – hardly the environment for innovation. Suddenly we come to Douglass North's ideas and the importance of the right institutional structures and value systems. Issues of trade reform and intellectual property rights, of trust and judgment, of cultural differences, all go to explain why some areas seem to have no problem in creating hot-spots, while others, particularly where governments interfere with (excessively tax and regulate) trade, are doomed to failure because they drive talent away.

Innovative firms cluster in hot-spots, the very concentration acting as a magnet for established innovators and a spur for new enterprise: witness the development of Silicon Valley, Hong Kong, Singapore, Dubai. The successful hot-spot engenders an institutional environment that mobilises intellectual talent and promotes and finances entrepreneurial activity, by delivering the right incentives in a society built on the right conventions. Then the elite of migrating global players will be convinced to stay, and a virtuous circle of success is ensured as their wealth is invested locally.

Different states in Europe have embarked on 'regulatory arbitrage' to tempt financial sector companies away from what are laughingly called their 'European partners.' By leveraging its tax advantages within the EU, Eire became the biggest exporter of software in the world – or rather re-exporter of software: Irish factories just shrink-wrap CDs holding other countries' software. That loophole will soon be closed, and then we'll see if the software industry continues or decamps. Inevitably the trend for EU-wide standardisation will undermine national legislation and taxation policies. However, not only will state be pitted against state, but also area against area, town against town, even suburb against suburb. As Daniel Bell so eloquently put it, "the nation-state is too small for the big things and too big for the small things." Some futurologists expect the number of states in the United Nations will increase from the present membership of 191 to over a thousand. Such shakeout trends can be seen as 'downsizing.' Territory in itself is a liability. Why waste resources subsidising large tracts of land filled with rusting industry and populated with the unemployed? To protect their wealth, rich areas will 'right-size,' ensuring a high proportion of wealth generating talent workers to wealth depleting service workers.

Fundamental to Coase's theory is the idea that property rights, rather than goods are being traded. What is at issue is how these rights, and the transaction of property rights, are costed and protected, and how conflicts over such resources can be resolved. North says that "institutions structure human interaction so we know how to deal with each other. They define the way markets work, whether a technology is worthwhile developing. Understand that structure and we'll understand the constraints we impose on ourselves." North emphasises the need to develop stable economic institutions, and stresses the importance of property rights, rules and laws (including taxation policies), and a judicial system, so that individual entrepreneurs and companies can be helped to help themselves.

Under these pressures, will European nation-states fragment? Or will they be artificially held together with the *Euro* as a form of elastoplast? Will Belgium break in two? What about Italy, Spain, France, and Germany? What about the United Kingdom that has never been truly united? The clamour for independence for Scotland and Wales, under the umbrella of the European Union, could soon become deafening. But rich areas too will be revolting; they see the advantage of dumping poor areas; the Czech Republic is far better off without those poor fools of Slovakia who demanded independence. How soon before the Home Counties realise the benefits of discarding that black hole for taxes north of Watford?

So can the Euro-zone become a hot-spot, a Smart Region, with a booming economy based on ICT? Are its leaders capable of accepting the need for new robust institutions "when groups in society see a possibility of availing themselves of profits that are impossible to realise under prevailing institutional conditions" (Douglass North)? Will they successfully answer the questions of who pays society's bills, how much they should pay, and for how much longer, against a background of the changing conditions I have been describing? Alan Greenspan predicts they're finished unless the EU finally leaves the Industrial Age and scraps its highly restrictive labour laws. (Some would say the CAP is stuck even earlier in the Agricultural Age, and the EU is badly in need of its own version of the Repeal of the Corn Laws.)

We must contrast the sentimentality of the European Union's vision of a Socialist "Information Society," against the hard-edged capitalist American Dream of an "Information Economy." Should we refer to the E-USSR, rather the EU? The European Union is just the Soviet Union with a forty-year time lag. The latest expansion of membership, the entry of Poland, Romania etc., not to mention Turkey, make collapse inevitable. The European (Soviet) Union will crumble in 2028. It's a simple matter of arithmetic – the original Soviet Union lasted from 1917 to 1989; the European version started in 1956.

The EU's outmoded collectivist and bureaucratic institutions, so steeped in the 'Factory Metaphor', are incompatible with the aspirations and expectations of the entrepreneurial networks that are creating the New Order of business. European politicians think that all businesses are run for their benefit, to pay for schemes that will buy them votes. This slime mould of popular socialism will always create a dependency culture that ultimately destroys innovation, precipitates the entry of organised crime into business, and undermines the ability to generate wealth.

As the OECD says: "low regulatory burdens enable US firms to start small scale, experiment, test the market with their business model, and, if successful expand rapidly. Moreover, if they do not succeed, the costs of failure are relatively limited." Can Europe (can a Britain sleepwalking into the Euro-zone) scrap its moribund institutions and compete; or are we on the verge of an unprecedented ICT brain drain of both individual talent and company-owned intellectual capital? And I have hardly mentioned China and India rapidly overtaking everyone on the outside! Perversely the international dynastic businesses born out of those countries' separate diasporas are using the institution of the 'family' to advantage in their assault on the world economy, an institution killed off long ago in the democratic West.

Both Britain and the Euro-zone face similar dire problems. With their supporting institutions (defined in the most general way) grounded in the Industrial Age, they are not capable of profiting from the new socio-economic conditions being created by new technology. As to whether Britain should scrap sterling and join the Euro, it may turn out that, as this author believes, we may be damned if we do, and damned if we don't, in that the institutional inertia behind both currencies cannot be diverted from failure.

As an afterthought, let me pose again the question: What do you get when you mix the British Pound (B£) with the EURO? The anagrammatic ROUB£E.

Tom McNally
Leader of the Liberal Democrats in the House of Lords

On a clear day you can see Europe

Towards the end of the third reading debate on the ratification of the Lisbon Treaty on 18 June, 2008, the then Lord president of the Council (and now British EU commissioner) Baroness Ashton quoted from a piece of campaign literature which had been circulated in Ireland. What she said moved me deeply and I quote it now because I feel it sums up my attitude to the great European adventure which has occupied centre stage during the whole of my political life. These were the words she quoted:

> "Europe isn't easy. It permeates day-to-day life, and like the Galway water system, is ignored unless it vanishes. It is boring. But it works. Imagine if one were to step through a tear in time, and appear in front of some prisoners in Auschwitz or Belsen. Imagine telling them of a Europe at peace, and democratic from Talin to Galway ... an elected Parliament and a guarantee that a Pole in Germany or a German in Malta or a Maltese in Sweden can stand up and say – I am an EU citizen, and I will be treated as an equal ... A Europe in which French and German ministers sit in joint cabinet sessions, elected in free elections ... They would call it fantasy. Yet every day 490 million people call it home."

I confess to being not a little moved by Baroness Ashton's words. To me the triumph of Europe has been to emerge from bloody, fratricidal conflict in the first half of the 20th century and build institutions on the basis of democracy and political negotiation. Europe's success stands as an example to other areas of conflict that even the longest and most deep seated of political enmities can be solved. The core Europe that bound up the wounds of war was the dream-child of Jean Monnet, often called the Father of Europe. I had the honour of working with Monsieur Monnet towards the end of his life. I remember once asking him what had been the driving force behind his dream. He replied, "I wanted to create something that made it impossible for Germany and France to go to war with each other ever again". The Monnet dream was to extend its influence in the 1970s by providing the stick and carrot which enabled Spain, Portugal and Greece to move from fascism in to the mainstream of European life. Europe was able to repeat the trick when the Berlin Wall came down and the new democracies of Eastern Europe, which emerged, saw the EU as the standard setter for their new institutions.

Now I am not so starry-eyed as to ignore the mistakes and missed opportunities that Europe has made over the last 50 years; but all the urban myths surrounding Brussels bureaucracy pale in to insignificance compared with the central triumph of replacing centuries of conflict by a co-operation which has brought both prosperity and influence to the people of Europe. There is not a single issue on the global agenda, from climate change to trade reform, from international terrorism to organised crime, which is not better and more effectively handled within a European framework.

Yet in Britain the debate about Europe has not changed during the now almost 50 years I have been involved. I remember a cartoon in the 1960s, when the then Conservative government had applied to join the Common Market. It showed British prime minister, Sir Alec Douglas-Home, standing at the door of a sports changing room. Inside can be seen all the leading statesmen of Europe pulling on football shirts and lacing up their football boots. Sir Alec is holding a cricket bat and wearing cricket whites. The cartoon is entitled "Joining the Game". Like all good cartoons it has a message of brutal simplicity. During most of the post-war period successive British governments, unwilling to face up to the post-war realities of diminished influence and power and self-deluded by the idea of a special relationship with the United States, consistently underestimated the sense of purpose of our European neighbours. As a result British Europeanism, such as it was, was based on expediency and force majeure rather than any vision or inner conviction.

The late Roy Jenkins used to compare Britain to a man on a railway platform hesitating about boarding a train. He would dither until the train began to move. Then, in Roy's words, "He scrambles aboard with as much dignity as he can muster – only to find that the best seats in the dining car have been taken". Those who knew Roy well will know how serious he judged missing the best seats in the dining car!

The other pattern of post war politics has been the habit of our major political parties to play the anti-Europe card when in opposition. In the 1960s, 70s and 80s the Labour Party moved from Gaitskell's defence of a thousand years of British History, to Wilson & Brown "not taking no for an answer", to "No to Europe on Tory terms", to renegotiation and referendum, to withdrawal without referendum (at which point I left the Labour Party).

It is difficult to believe now that it was the Conservatives who took us in to Europe under Mr Heath and vastly extended the competences of the Union in the 80s under Mrs Thatcher or that the Lady was removed from office mainly because of her anti-Europeanism. The Conservatives run scared of UKIP and associate themselves in Strasbourg with a rag-bag of parties beyond the pale of the major centre-right governing parties. It is all very depressing. If there is a change of Government we will go through the usual reality check for the Conservatives; but only after maximum damage is done to British interests whilst another set of ministers travel the learning curve.

Perhaps it will need another "in or out" referendum to smoke out those who know Britain has to be at the heart of Europe; but in the meantime are happy to mop up any xenophobic or little-Englander votes that are going. In many ways I am more confident than when I started on my European journey as a student in the early 60s that this country can best influence for the good the issues facing the world by playing a full hearted part in Europe. As I have already indicated, I can think of no challenge facing this country which is easier to face outside the EU. I have been blessed by three children who will live most of their lives in the 21st century. I am proud of being part of a political generation which got Britain into Europe and kept her there. I sometimes feel like an old gunfighter, ready to strap my guns on for one more show-down if need be. I would much prefer that my children grew up in their European home as citizens proud of their country; but equally proud to be part of a Europe of peace, prosperity and influence.

* * * * *

Also available from Shoehorn

SAVING THE EUROPEAN UNION
The Logic of the Lisbon Treaty
by Andrew Duff

This book explains and justifies the EU's Treaty of Lisbon. It is the first accurate and comprehensive description of what the entry into force of Lisbon treaty will mean. It provides logical answers both to those pro-Europeans who claim that Lisbon is of little importance and to those anti-Europeans who oppose further integration.

Tony Barber, writing in the *Financial Times,* described the book as *"an excellent introduction to the Lisbon treaty and to the challenges facing today's EU. Friends and foes alike of the EU will benefit from reading it. Duff is one of the European Parliament's top constitutional affairs experts, and he writes clean, crisp prose."*

Lightning Source UK Ltd.
Milton Keynes UK
07 November 2009

145933UK00001B/13/P

9 781907 149078